OUT OF ORDER!

The very Unofficial Vermont State House Archives

Frank Germaine
1991

OUT OF ORDER!

The very Unofficial Vermont State House Archives

by Bill Mares and Frank Bryan

Illustrated by Don Hooper

THE NEW ENGLAND PRESS
Shelburne, Vermont

ISBN 0-933050-88-7
Library of Congress Card number: 91-066745
Design by Andrea Gray

For additional copies of this book or for a catalog of our other
New England titles, please write:

The New England Press
P.O. Box 575
Shelburne, VT 05482

ACKNOWLEDGMENTS

Scores of people contributed to this book. For their help, encouragement, and stories we would like to thank: Tom Slayton, Steve Terry, Howard Coffin, Nick Marro, John Irwin, Mark MacDonald, Don Hooper, Bob Kinsey, Todd Shapera, Father Philip Branon, Harvey Carter, Ann Harroun, Bill Keogh, Joyce Lindamood, Walt Moore, Lloyd Selby, Steve Reynes, Paul Poirier, Ralph Wright, Madeleine Kunin, Steve Morse, "Peanut" Kennedy, Jack Candon, Bob Stannard, John Kenneth Galbraith, Gene Godt, Reid Lefevre, *The Burlington Free Press*, *The Rutland Herald*, Kendall Wild, Charlie Morrissey, T. Garry Buckley, John McClaughry, M. Dickey Drysdale, Art Sanborn, Ed Zuccaro, Louie Berney, Scott Skinner, Mary Evelti, Norm Runnion, Peter Freyne, Marshall Dimock, Perry Waite, Gilly Godnick, Ann Seibert, Peter Allendorf, Barbara Grimes, Mike Barnes, Howard Dean, Edgar May, Bill Talbott, Phil Hoff, Ralph Baker, Paul Hannan, Merrill Perley, Raul Hilberg, James Pacy, and Ken Walker.

Special thanks go to Bob Picher and Keith Wallace.

CONTENTS

INTRODUCTION

VERN FLECKMER, a lanky State House custodian, settled deeper into one of the red velvet seats that bracketed the Speaker's podium in the Vermont House of Representatives. It was mid-June. The legislature had departed the week before, four weeks beyond its scheduled adjournment. A week earlier, the 150 seats had been filled with scheming, deal-making legislators. Lobbyists had prowled the hallways, and legislative staff members had rushed to and fro carrying revised bills. The one or two civilians looking on had been as lonely as Yankee fans in Fenway.

Now the great oval room with its massive chandelier was empty—happily so, thought Vern. In the twenty years he had worked in the State House, this was the most raucous and ragged legislative retreat he had seen. One of these days, he thought, those people will stay in session for the whole year.

He closed his eyes. The peace and quiet were welcome. He looked forward to having six months to himself, disturbed only by a few committee meetings and a trickle of tourists. . . .

"Fleckmer, what are you doing?" boomed a voice from across the hall. "Checking your eyes for light leaks?"

Vern cracked open one eye. It was Chet Tams, an ex-Marine, ex-high school teacher, ex-legislator, and the current assistant sergeant-at-arms.

Now done out of his nap, Vern roused himself and stretched. He'd grown up on a farm in Barre Town, since cut in half by the Interstate. After working in a paint store in Barre for a few years, he had found a custodian's job with the state. He'd worked in several government buildings in Montpelier, but he liked the State House best.

He shambled over to the podium. The gavel was gone. The microphones were dead, but not the memories that

washed over him like the smell of coffee and bacon at deer camp.

He looked out at the seats from behind the podium. He could remember legislators who had been so confused, they voted against their own motions. He remembered proponents arguing among themselves, and in one unforgettable case, a member, Representative Daniel DeBonis of Poultney, even interrogating himself.

"Boy, has this place changed," Vern remarked to Chet. "Twenty years ago, the big fights were between Republicans and Republicans. Back then, Democrats were about as rare as hen's teeth. Like that story about the two guys walking through the cemetery. They see a tombstone with the inscription, 'Here lies a good man and a Democrat.' And one man says to the other: 'I wonder why they buried those two together.'"

"The Democrats sure run this place now!" said Chet, laughing.

"Yeah, they come up here thinking they have a blank check to change every law they can find. Their attitude is: '*Something* gotta be done. *This here* is something. Therefore, we gotta do *this*!'"

"Ah, Vern, you're just sore because the Republicans have lost the speakership four times in a row even though they've had a majority in the House the whole time! If the Democrats had come up here and done nothing, you would have criticized them for wasting time. If you don't like this job, you can always tell the state to shove it and go back to the paint store."

"Funny thing is, I *do* like the job," said Vern. "It's fun to watch people getting taken down a peg. I heard one guy say of another: 'Old Torbert there is like the bottom half of a double boiler—all steamed up and doesn't know what's cooking.' Or take the time Vince Illuzzi and Bob Harris were the last people in the State House one night.

3

They got trapped by the new self-locking doors and couldn't get out. They finally had to kick out a glass window to escape. When Bob Stannard heard about it, he nailed 'em: 'We'll have to pass a new law just for those two guys—*breaking and exiting!*'"

"Now you're talking, Vern. Where else can you work, where you can watch a hundred and eighty people making fools of themselves every day? Where else do you get to see people soar so high and be brought so low so fast?"

"Amen to that. These legislators mean well, though. They're not idiots, or at least most of them aren't. They try hard, but they keep tying their own shoelaces together

and falling down. Over the years I've been collecting stories about politicians from all over Vermont. It's amazing what you pick up when you keep your mouth shut and your ears open."

Chet looked at Vern. "That's great. But what are you going to do with them? Make posters? Become a toastmaster? Write a silly book like Mares and that other guy? What was that called? *Real Vermonters Don't Shoot Goats?*"

"No, it's *Real Vermonters Don't Drink Goats' Milk* and the other guy was Bryan. I have that book, but I don't know about writing a book myself. I haven't decided," Vern said shyly.

Chet was curious now. "Where do you keep these tales?" he asked.

"You really want to know?" Vern was torn. He had never shown the stories to anyone—they were a secret—but he ached to tell Chet about them.

"Sure I do."

"Okay, I'll show you, if you'll keep them a secret."

Vern led the way out of the House chamber and out into the anteroom, where numerous lobbying groups—from Vermont Right to Life to Planned Parenthood, from the Vermont Trappers Association to the Friends of Animals—competed for attention and support at various times during the legislative session. The pair descended two flights of iron stairs painted battleship gray. In the basement, Vern and Chet entered the men's bathroom.

It had tile floors and ten urinals with marble slab dividers between them. There were ten stalls with oak doors and zinc coat racks, handsome porcelain basins, and smoked-glass light fixtures.

"Every time I come in here," said Chet, "I think I've gone back a hundred years. If the women in the legislature knew about these quarters, there'd be a revolution."

Vern led Chet to the far end of the room. There, in the dim light cast by a dust-covered bulb, were stacks of cardboard boxes, cabinets loaded with detergents, solvents, and paper towels, and an arsenal of mops and brooms. The smell of disinfectant hung heavy in the air.

"Every time I write down a story, I bring it down here and stuff it in this box," Vern explained. "Most of them are about the legislature, but I've picked up some other stuff as well. I also have some real classics that happened before I got here but are still talked about even now."

Sure enough, stuck behind the rolls of toilet paper and the light bulbs was a brown tin box about nine inches square. Vern undid the clasp and opened the box. There, like stuffing in a Thanksgiving turkey, were scores of pieces of paper. Some were handwritten, some were pages from the House and Senate journals, some were typed poems.

Vern pulled out a couple of pieces of paper and proffered them to Chet.

You three guys sure make a pair,

one read, and another:

There's a rotten egg in every barrel of apples.

"Those are from Gilly Godnick," explained Vern. "He was always saying that sort of thing."

Chet pulled out another.

The three great lies of today are:
(A) Your check is in the mail; (B) One size fits all; and (C) I'm from Washington and I'm here to help you.

"Edgar May said that once, when the Senate Appropriations Committee had to cut a lot from the budget," said Vern.

6

"Here's one about a former Speaker of the House, John S. Burgess. The *S* was supposed to stand for *slow*. Former lieutenant governor Tom Hayes once said: 'Jack Burgess is so slow that if he had been presiding at the Last Supper, our Lord would be with us today!'"

Chet burst out laughing.

"Here's one more," said Vern.

> A Flatlander comes into the town clerk's office in Hartford, Hancock, or Halifax and demands to have the clerk look at a deed. The clerk is already waiting on one person and asks the gentleman to take a seat.
>
> The man fumes at this lack of respect. 'Don't you know who I am? I'm president of this and trustee of that. . . . '
>
> 'Well, then,' said the clerk, 'Take two seats.'

"Okay, time to get back to work," said Vern, taking the papers back from Chet. He put them into the box, closed the lid, and slid the box out of sight behind the toilet paper.

"Now promise me you'll keep this a secret. In fact, just forget you ever saw these stories," said Vern, as the pair mounted the stairs.

"What about the rest of them?" asked Chet. "Won't you give me a chance to read them?"

"Nope. Maybe after I've figured what to do with them, and after I've collected a lot more, but that'll be a long, long time."

"Well, let me know if you want someone to read them."

"Okay."

And that's how it all began—in the basement men's room at the State House.

CAMPAIGNS

"WELL, IT'S THE BUDDING AUTHOR!" Vern set down his coffee cup at the Whole Donut cafe and waited for the hearty back slap he knew Chet would deliver. Thump! The coffee shook.

"Didn't spill any coffee today!" said Chet as he slipped into the opposite seat. His sunburned face bobbed like an apple atop a blue golf shirt.

Having coffee together at the State House was a habit with the pair, but during the summer they didn't see much of each other.

"And how is the book going on this fine summer morning?"

"Oh, the book's on vacation," said Vern. "Not much going on up at the State House—most people are out campaigning."

"You ought to have some good stories from the campaign trail," Chet offered. "I can remember the first time I ran. I kept putting it off. I kept asking myself: What did I have to offer the people? How would I solve the problem of school aid, or falling bridges, or welfare? But then I looked at my opponent and I thought: 'I'm at least as good as he is.'"

9

"And you never, never forgot it!" Vern observed dryly.

"Hey, that's not what I meant!" Chet replied testily. *You* never ran. *You* never put your ego on the line. *You* never spent night after night ringing doorbells and going to meetings and begging for votes."

"Come on, Chet. You chose to run. No one forced you."

"That's true," admitted Chet, "but I had no idea of what I was getting into. Campaigning is brutal—I never worked so hard at anything in my life. Phil Hoff once said: 'At the end of a race, if you still care who won, you haven't worked hard enough.'"

"Do you remember when Howard Dean announced he would run for lieutenant governor back in 1986 against Peter Smith, the incumbent?" continued Chet. "Then Smith decided to run against Governor Kunin. Within two days, eight other possible candidates were mentioned in the press, all with more experience than Howard. Representative Jack Candon watched this rush to the starting gate and said: 'Howard Dean is like the first soldier to hit the barbed wire—heroic, but he gets trampled by those who follow.'"

"Yeah, some pretty weird things happen on the trail," replied Vern. "Bill Mares up in Burlington told me that when he was campaigning in his first term, he went into an apartment filled with used tires and furniture and a stereo blasting away. In one corner was a terrarium with—get this—a huge boa constrictor eating a white mouse. The man who lived there wanted to register to vote. 'Don't worry about the snake,' the man said. But Mares wasn't sure. He said he'd never forget standing to administer the Freeman's Oath while he watched the mouse's rear legs disappear down the snake's throat."

Chet laughed, then turned serious. "You know, my offer of help with the book is still good. From where I

11

sit in the sergeant-at-arms office, it's like a general store for gossip and rumor. I could see if other people have stories that should be included. We'll call them 'guest appearances' or something like that. I'll collect them, and I'll let you dump them in your strongbox—but only if you let me read the rest of your stories."

Vern was silent for a moment. "No, I don't think I'm ready. I don't think I have enough. When I do, I'll let you know. Yeah, I could probably use a hand. Spelling and writing are not my high cards."

"Well, you think about it," said Chet as he rose to leave. "Here's one you ought to put in the box. I wrote up my favorite version of an old story that Representative Foley used to tell." And he handed Vern a piece of paper.

> The election officials were counting ballots in an Orange County town forty years ago. After piling up a stack of Republican ballots three inches high, they found a Democratic vote. Again, a host of Republican votes was followed by a solitary Democratic ballot.
>
> 'Humpf!' said one election commissioner, 'that S.O.B. must have voted twice!'

Vern smiled as he finished off his coffee.

Eating Humble Pie

Democrat Frank Branon ran for governor in 1954, and at that time it was tough to be a Democrat. There hadn't been a Democratic governor in Vermont in almost a hundred years, and it appeared the next one was equally far in the future.

But Branon was a game campaigner, and he traveled the state tirelessly. One night in mid-October, he and his wife found themselves at a church supper in Fairfax. Branon bolted his food and then began his appeal to the sober and somber group. Meanwhile, his wife settled in with a group of women toward the back of the hall.

Branon spoke well and coaxed some smiles and chuckles from the group. When he finished, Mrs. Branon thought the time was probably ripe for her appeal.

She leaned across the table and whispered to the woman who had seemed the most enthusiastic during the speech: "Excuse me—I'd sure appreciate it if you could support my husband in the election."

"Oh, no!" said the lady, "we couldn't do *that*. We've been Vermonters all our lives!"

In the Nick of Time

During one of his campaigns, Representative Lloyd Selby (R-Derby) drove up to a small collection of houses on a bare windswept hillside. He parked in the first driveway, which was cluttered with children's toys and a couple of abandoned cars. As he approached the house, he noticed a large Doberman pinscher sitting near the porch. Suddenly the dog leaped up and bulleted toward Selby. Moving as quickly as a sixty-five-year-old can, he scrammed back to the car and got inside a microsecond before the dog crashed against the door.

For a few moments Selby sat there puffing deep breaths of relief. The dog snarled a few times and returned to its post. Once he had recovered, Selby looked up and around to see if anyone had seen his ragged retreat. Sure enough, a neighbor was working on his car. He caught Selby's eye, waved, and called out cheerfully, "You're lucky. Wait 'til you meet the lady who owns him!"

Are You Running with Me, Jesus?

When Bill Mares first ran for election, a friend advised him to become a notary public so that he could register voters as he campaigned. She said that most of the people whom he registered, *if* they voted, would vote for him. In his primary campaign, as it turned out, he registered more than 130 people, a hefty number of potential supporters.

So he added a final sentence to his standard pitch at the door. It went as follows:

"Hello, I'm Bill Mares, and I'm running as a Democrat for the state House of Representatives. If you're registered to vote, I hope you'll consider me on Primary Day, September tenth." Then he would offer his flier.

At one particular duplex on Maple Street in Burlington, a young woman came to the door. She looked harried, and Mares could hear the cries of two small children in the background.

When he finished his spiel, she fixed him with a steely look and then asked:

"Was Jesus registered?"

"Uh, er—um, I don't know," Mares responded.

"Well, if you can show me that Christ voted, then I'll register." And she firmly shut the door.

As usually happens, Mares thought of a reply five minutes later—"Well, his parents had to go to Bethlehem to pay taxes; those were probably poll taxes," he should have said.

But of course he didn't.

☆ ☆ ☆ ☆ GUEST APPEARANCE ☆ ☆ ☆ ☆

Tips for Would-Be Vermont Pols*
Dick McCormack

1. Don't talk up your agricultural policy with farmers unless you're a farmer. They've heard it all before.

2. Don't drink coffee in your car on your way to a meeting while wearing your only clean pants.

3. Shave your beard. Believe it or not, there are folks for whom it's a problem. (My response—"Hey, I'm running for Senate, not Miss America"—is clever but probably hasn't gotten me one vote.)

4. Don't argue with people who obviously despise you and your politics. Your job is to get votes, not argue for the fun of it. (I've never once obeyed this rule.)

5. Don't guess the sex of someone's baby. There's a 90 percent chance you'll guess wrong.

6. Even if your personal ethics would allow you to tell people what you think they want to hear, don't. People rarely think what you think they think.

7. Don't try to do too much in one day. You simply can't get from Ludlow to Norwich in twenty minutes no matter what your schedule says.

8. Have someone else proofread your pamphlets. You'll see what you expect to see whether it's there or not. (I personally approved a run of 10,000 pamphlets with a glaring typo.)

9. Keep your other job.

*From *North by Northeast*, a publication of Vermont Public Radio, December 1988

The Wright Choice

In the summer of 1984, House Democratic leader Ralph Wright was campaigning all over the state, both for the speakership and to find Democratic candidates for House races.

He called up to the town of Franklin to reach a potential candidate he had heard about. Apparently, there was something wrong with the phone line, and Wright couldn't get through. He called the operator.

A vaguely familiar male voice came on the line. "May I help you?"

Wright said he wanted to reach so-and-so.

"I'll put you right through, Ralph."

Wright was nonplussed. "Who is this?" he growled.

"Hugh Gates," said the man. Gates was the owner of the Franklin Telephone Company, and the incumbent Republican state representative.

"Hey, get off the line," said Wright. "I'm trying to find someone to run against you!"

Right on the Money

It was January 1971, and Representative Walter "Peanut" Kennedy (R-Chelsea) was running for Speaker of the House. Kennedy was confident that he would win, but that was not good enough for the reporters. How many votes would he get? they kept asking.

Finally, shortly before the vote, Kennedy said, "Okay, I'll tell you. I'll get ninety-two votes." But he wouldn't say how he could be so specific.

The election came, and, as Kennedy had predicted, he got ninety-two votes. The reporters were flabbergasted. They gathered around to ask how he had been so sure.

"Well," he said. "First, I counted all the Republicans who said they would vote for me. Then I counted the Democrats who I thought would vote for me. And I didn't ask any of them to make a commitment.

"Then I took away the ones who had said they would vote for me but I knew wouldn't. I subtracted ten percent for erosion, and that's how I arrived at ninety-two."

How Jaundiced a Candidate Can Become

A Burlington representative was campaigning with another aspirant in a two-person district. They came to a house on Scarff Avenue, and the incumbent walked past the door without stopping. The novice asked why the other had not rung the bell.

"The man who lived there died a few months ago."

"That's too bad," said the sympathetic candidate.

"Oh, he didn't vote anyway!" replied the veteran, eyeing the next door.

Getting to Know You

Statewide campaigns are grueling affairs—sixteen-, eighteen-, or twenty-hour days of small speeches, impromptu gatherings, indigestible food, hundreds of indistinguishable faces, the nattering press. The resulting exhaustion of the candidates can lead not just to slips but to downright embarrassment.

As the 1976 U.S. senatorial race ground to a close, Senator Robert Stafford was campaigning in Ludlow. He waded through still another reception crowd and paused to shake hands with an attractive woman wearing a Stafford button.

"Hi, I'm Bob Stafford," he said.

"I know," the woman replied. "I'm your wife."

The Fine Art of Disdaining

In one of his campaigns, Senator George Aiken was hotly but distantly pursued by a now-forgotten opponent. Throughout the race, Aiken hardly acknowledged the man's existence. The fellow became infuriated. Aiken, he howled, was too proud or too cowardly—or both—to debate him.

After the press repeatedly asked him for a response, Aiken finally replied, "The *eagle* does not talk to the *sparrow*."

(There's a Latin aphorism from which this remark must come: *Aequilla non capet mosces*—"The eagle does not hunt flies.")

A Case of Mistaken Identity

The setting was a central Vermont Grange Hall, where a couple of dozen Grangers had gathered to hear seven candidates make their respective pitches. By the time the sixth speaker began his dissertation, half the audience was dozing.

Undaunted, Representative Ralph Baker, a Randolph Republican, plowed ahead to report on his community service work.

"Furthermore, I have been spending a good deal of time recently working with students at the high school on a special project. I have started a fencing club. Equipment was hard to find, but the technical college had some stored away that wasn't too rusty."

A shiver of excitement went through the crowd. Eyes opened, chairs scraped. There were whispers back and forth: "Fencing, eh? 'Bout time that school taught something worthwhile."

Baker continued: "And before the year is out, we hope to have some competition with other schools."

The crowd looked quizzical.

"And if this really catches on," said Baker, hitting his stride, "we may be able to get some modern masks and chest protectors."

Slowly, it dawned on the crowd. "Fencing"—one man poked at another—"you know, swords." The rest looked crestfallen. Then came one loud whisper, "What'd you expect—something practical?"

Words, Words, Words

In 1982, one William J. Leahy (no relation of U.S. Senator Patrick J. Leahy) ran for sheriff of Franklin County. His campaign posters promised "Compassion, Empathy, and Rhetoric." Even some of his supporters scratched their heads about the last word. Did Leahy know the English language?

"Of course," he replied. "Rhetoric means the art of effective communications. I used the word deliberately so that people would have a reason to ask me about it and I could explain why I am running."

Apparently, not enough people were intrigued or curious about his explanation, for on Election Day, he lost.

A Case of Fowl Play?

In 1982, obstetrician Dr. John Maeck ran for Chittenden County senator as a Republican. When he tried to add the title "Dr." to his name on the ballot, Secretary of State James Douglas told him it violated the election laws. It was Democratic senatorial candidate Douglas Racine who had called Douglas's attention to the offense.

Maeck was incensed. "But I *delivered* the son-of-a-gun!" he fumed, referring to Racine.

"No, he didn't " replied Racine. Although Maeck *was* Racine's mother's obstetrician, he had apparently gone duck hunting on the day Racine arrived and another doctor attended.

"I finally got back at him for taking the day off," said Racine.

Advice from the Ages

Incumbent Bennington County Senator Harvey Carter and newcomer Seth Bongartz were running as a team in the election of 1986. One day they drove to West Rupert to the last farm before the border.

The farm belonged to a town patriarch whose family had owned the farm for several generations. The man was now in his eighties and, on doctor's orders, was too old to drive a tractor. Although his body was frail, his mind and wit were robust. The pair found him in his living room resting in an easy chair. Happy to have visitors, he engaged them in a wide-ranging conversation that roamed from the price of grain to doings in Rupert to the drought that was then ravaging the American Southeast.

"You know, we've had some pretty bad droughts in Vermont," he said.

Carter and Bongartz rushed to nod. "Yes, we know."

The old man was quiet for a minute. Then he raised himself up out of the lounger and observed, "Come to think of it, droughts are a lot like snow and sex."

"Oh, how so?" asked the eager pair.

"Well, you're never sure how much you'll get, or how long it will last."

In Orbit with Jerry Brown

In 1980, California governor Jerry Brown brought to Vermont his quixotic campaign for president.

At his weekly press conference, Vermont governor Richard Snelling was asked what he thought of the idiosyncratic Brown, who was nicknamed "Governor Space Cadet." Snelling, who had met Brown at several National Governors conferences, didn't bite.

"I don't mind being around Governor Brown. I've been in buildings with him several times, and they didn't fall down. I'm even willing to be on the same spaceship with him."

A Man of Few Words

Politicians are supposed to be long-winded. In 1980, Representative Donald Moore (R-Shrewsbury) put the lie to that cliché. Called by a reporter and asked if he planned to run for reelection, he replied, "Yes." Asked further if he had any pet legislation he planned to work on or introduce, he said, "Nope."

Getting the Names Straight

When Democrat M. Jerome "Jerry" Diamond ran for attorney general in 1974, his two opponents were the incumbent, Republican Kimberly Cheney, and Liberty Union candidate Peter Diamondstone.

Diamond was worried that voters, reporters, and debate moderators would confuse him with Diamondstone. Thus, at one of the first face-to-face debates, Diamond's first words were: "I want to make one thing perfectly clear: My name is not Peter Diamondstone; it's Jerry Diamondstone . . . er Diamond!"

Several minutes later, when it was Cheney's turn, he said, "My name is Kimberly Cheney—and I've never forgotten it."

Just Trying to Help . . .

Republican John McClaughry—former state representative, longtime Kirby moderator, and later state senator—should have known better.

In July 1986, McClaughry offered some unsolicited campaign advice to Anthony Doria of South Royalton, who was running against former governor Richard Snelling for the Republican nomination to challenge incumbent U.S. Senator Patrick Leahy. In the letter, McClaughry, a founder of the conservative Vermont Republican Assembly, urged Doria to describe Snelling as the "fat guy," Leahy as the "bald guy," and himself, Doria, as the "little guy," who supported President Reagan on his Central American policy.

Doria lost to Snelling in the primary, and he announced he would run as an independent. A few days later, McClaughry held a news conference to urge Doria not to run; it would diminish Republican prospects, he said.

A few days after that, Doria called his *own* press conference to reject McClaughry's recommendation and to display the letter. Doria, who is short, balding, and if not fat, then at least stout, said he couldn't follow the proffered advice because "I'm all three!"

Hopes Dashed

For weeks, Stephen Reynes of Pomfret had been trying to launch his first campaign for the Vermont House. Like most candidates-to-be, he was plagued by a mixture of shyness, nervousness, and lethargy. Finally, on July 4, 1982, he decided *this is the day*. A potluck supper at a

Pomfret church would be a good place to begin. Once he arrived at the church, he stood at the entrance for five minutes while he figured out how to introduce himself.

Finally, he began. "Hello, I'm Steve Reynes, and I'm running for the legislature." For five or ten minutes, the people walking past gave him polite nods or blank stares.

Then up strode a man about sixty—friendly, curious—who said, "What do you think about the legislature controlling the deer herd?" Happy that someone had shown an interest, Reynes gave him a detailed answer.

"Well, then, what do you think about state aid to education?"

An invigorated Reynes offered his solution to this perennial problem.

"And the state budget, highway construction, the drinking age?" followed from this friendly inquisitor.

By now Reynes was excited. Here was someone who was alert, knowledgeable, and apparently appreciative of his answers. This man, because of his intelligence, was probably influential with lots of voters.

Reynes asked the man his name. "Oh, I don't like to give my name to politicians." Reynes tried again. "Where do you live?" The man would rather not say. Reynes was a bit surprised but thought the man was probably one of those self-contained Vermonters. Reynes wished the man well and asked for his support on Election Day.

No one else came by, so Reynes turned around to buy a ticket for dinner. It surprised him to see that the ticket seller was none other than his opponent, the incumbent representative. She wore a dark look.

"I don't think you should be campaigning here at this supper," she hissed. "And *besides*, my husband won't vote for you, anyway!"

Endangered Political Species

Electricity is so much a part of our lives these days, and it has been for so long, that most of us can hardly imagine the excitement its arrival engendered.

Former state representative and Essex County sheriff John Irwin recalled that event in the towns of Granby and Victory.

"In 1960, there was a big celebration up there to welcome the coming of power to those two towns.

"Bill Meyer of Pawlet was running for reelection to Congress on the Democratic slate. He wrote a letter to us 'inviting himself' to visit the Holiday in the Hills program to make his pitch.

"A friend and I decided to make his visit memorable. We found an old bear trap, a felt boot, and a weathered cow's leg bone. We set the bone in the boot in the trap and placed the whole thing at the corner of the Cook Shack, where Meyer was supposed to be dropped off. Next to the boot we put a sign that read, 'The last Democrat in Granby.'

"Well, when Meyer arrived, he didn't blink. He walked right over to the display, put one of his buttons on the boot, and then started shaking every hand he could find."

Chasing the Voters

In 1986, two-term state representative Howard Dean (D-Burlington) launched his campaign for lieutenant governor. In many local communities he asked the help of fellow legislators. One of these was Mark MacDonald (D-Williamstown).

"I had agreed to take Howard around Williamstown to meet some farmers," MacDonald recalled. "We drove some of the back roads and finally stopped at one farm where we could see this guy way out in the field tedding hay. Howard wanted to go meet him. So we got out of the car and started walking across the field. About half-way there, I suddenly realized this farmer was a woman.

"Then, when we got closer, I could see her reaching behind her to pull out some cloth. Damned if she wasn't shirtless. I knelt down to tie my shoe.

"I hollered to Howard, but he was too intent on jumping windrows and getting to this voter. I could see the tractor laying down the crookedest windrow you ever saw as she tried to drive and put her shirt on at the same time.

"When Howard got about twenty feet from her, he looked up, and she only had a couple of buttons done. He stopped in his tracks and turned around. She stopped the tractor and finished buttoning her shirt. Howard was blushing, but he still managed to make his campaign pitch."

Three Strikes and You're Out

During that same campaign, Dean stopped at the general store in Fairlee. When he announced his mission to the octogenarian store owner, the man looked him up and down.

"Where you from?" he asked.

"Burlington," Dean replied.

"That's one. Were you born in Vermont?"

"No," admitted Dean.

"That's two. Now are you a Republican or a Democrat?"

"Democrat," said Dean.

"That's three. Nice to meet you." And he pointed toward the door.

Women's Liberation—Vermont Style

In 1974, Democrat Christine Hadsel decided to run for the House of Representatives from the town of St. Johnsbury. Not only was she new to the district, she was the first Democratic woman in memory to run. Undaunted, she spent the fall ringing every doorbell in the town.

Towards the end of the race, Walter "Peanut" Kennedy, the Republican candidate for governor, came to town to campaign for himself and his fellow Republicans. To a gathering of the faithful, he joked that he didn't see any problems ahead for "my good friend Ed Crane [the incumbent] because his opponent is some woman afraid to use her own name."

When told of the remark, the feisty Hadsel replied that she *was* using her own name—and what's more, she let her husband, Bill Mares, use *his* own name as well!

What's In a Name?

The late Robert Babcock ran for governor in the Republican primary of 1960 and lost to F. Ray Keyser, Jr. At the time he was a professor of political science at the University of Vermont. One day he offered colleague Raul Hilberg an explanation of his loss.

"Want to know how I lost the race, Raul?"

"How?"

"I was campaigning over in Chelsea. A reporter asked me what I was going to do about brucellosis, and I said, 'Who's that?'"

P E O P L E

ON THE FIRST DAY OF THE NEW SESSION, the lobby of the State House was jammed with legislators, lobbyists, staff, media, and citizens. Awaiting the governor's inauguration, they milled about and greeted one another like long-lost friends. The bust of Lincoln wore a bemused look as people darted this way and that. In a painting outside the sergeant-at-arms' office, Montpelier-born Admiral George Dewey presided over real shot and shell from the battle of Manila Bay.

Vern was mopping up the results of a collision between two senators and their respective coffee cups.

"Hey, Vern—you glad the kids are back at school?" yelled Chet from the sergeant-at-arms' office. Fleckmer grimaced, then grinned.

Chet stepped out of the office and wove through a covey of legislative pages, who were simultaneously proud and self-conscious in their new bright green blazers.

While Vern paused to rest his chin on the mop handle, Chet observed:

"You know, Vern, there's a lot more variety in this legislative crowd than when I was up here fifteen years ago."

"More women, fewer farmers, the way I count," said the laconic Fleckmer.

"Yeah, that's so, but there's a sprinkling of almost everyone here—bankers, lawyers, doctors, teachers, farmers, insurance agents, retirees. There's even a goat farmer, a railroad worker, and a clown. It's a pretty good cross-section of the general population."

"One lawyer is too many, far as I'm concerned," growled Vern. "You remember last year when Glendon King of Northfield was up here? He needed to ask for a lawyer's opinion about a tax bill. He asked Speaker Wright if he could interrogate Edward Zuccaro, a representative from St. Johnsbury who is a lawyer. 'Oh, the barrister?' asked Wright. 'No, I won't embarrass him,' said King, who couldn't hear very well."

"I think the legislature is representative of the public out there. The only difference is that politicians have bigger egos."

"But usually there's someone who can puncture their balloons. Reid LeFevre was great at this. Once there was a debate about whether to knock off members' pay when they had unexcused absences. He killed the bill with one remark: 'Mr. Speaker, there are members of the House who serve *most* generously when they are absent from this chamber!'"

"Yeah, but there are also members who take themselves down a peg," added Chet. "When he heard someone list the legislators whose marriages had broken up during their Montpelier service, John Orzell, an eighteen-year veteran with his marriage still intact, observed, 'Well, it's a good thing I wasn't born good-looking!'"

"I never heard that one. You write those down. I may have to let you see the rest of these stories," said Vern.

"King Reid"

"King Reid" Lefevre (R-Manchester) served in the House and Senate for twenty-one years. He was a big man who looked like H. L. Mencken, and he revered the English language in the same way. He had a kindred wit to Mencken, and there was a bit of P. T. Barnum in him, too. This is perhaps not surprising, since he owned a circus that traveled around the East when the legislature was not in session. In 1947, he brought his circus to the State House and put a sign up over the door: "This way to the Monkey House."

Lefevre once attended a Republican fund raiser that offered the usual rubber chicken, tired peas, pasty potatoes, and wavering Jello. At the end of the meal, a mimeographed sheet was passed around. Each person was asked to write down the most crucial short-term and long-term problems facing the state Republican party.

To the first question he wrote: "Indigestion."

To the second he wrote: "Acute indigestion."

Lefevre could also be devastating on the floor of the House. He once described a fellow member thus: "He has an insufficiency disguised as incompetence."

And no one else could stop a debate about the evils of salting the highways by saying, "Mr. Speaker, I think we should stop arguing about the brine on the road before we all get pickled."

The Car Dealer as Speaker

In 1972, members of the House were treated to a rare spectacle—Speaker Walter Kennedy came down from the podium to speak against a bill. The issue was a proposal by Representative Marshall Whitten of Bennington to raise the state's take from the Pownal race track. Kennedy, no supporter of the track or of gambling in general, said, however, that he didn't think it fair to change the rules in the middle of the game by increasing the state's cut of the profits.

On the day the bill was reported to the House floor, Kennedy turned the gavel over to Speaker *pro tem* Hancock and began his remarks with the following lines: "I want you all to know I believe in honesty, even though I am both a politician and a car dealer."

(After the laughter subsided, Kennedy went on to argue cogently [and successfully] that the bill be defeated.)

Caveat Taxpayer
F. Eugene Godt

F. Eugene Godt, a Brookline auditor and retired jour-nalist, served three terms in the legislature in the 1980s, where his avuncular wit and compassion were much prized. In 1974, Godt wrote the following letter to a Con-necticut resident who owned property in Brookline. Only the names have been changed:

February 26, 1974

Dear Mr. Drayton,

Since you are now officially a taxpayer in and for the Town of Brookline, Vermont, and thus may participate in our Town Meeting the night of March 5, 1974, I thought it only fair that you receive a special annotated copy of the formal Town Report. It is enclosed.

I should call your attention to the following pages and items in the Report:

Page 3. You will note that I am one of the three Town Auditors. It is a position of some responsi-bility but small financial reward (see page 6).

Now turn to page 5, and consider the Dog Li-cense matter. In 1972 we reported 53 dogs with a gross total receipt of $103.00, which compares unfavorably with the current report of 57 dogs with a gross receipt of $91.00. Thus 8% more dogs brought in 11.6% less profit. If you carry this to its obvious conclusion, adding dogs and losing revenue, there will come a time when we will be hip deep in free dogs.

However, you will immediately be aware of the new classification "spayed female dogs (delin-quent)." What more appropriate way to turn a modest dollar than to provide a delinquent spayed female or two in the present era of increasing tension? That's what is called a rhetorical question, upon which you may reflect while I tell you that my fellow Auditor, Mrs. Eric Temple, calls these altered animals "sprayed females," which conjures up an interesting mental image.

Under "Payments" on the Report note the item "Helen Howe Bridge painting: $488.23." The Helen Howe Bridge spans Grassy Brook down south of Matt Nau's place, and is not quite as long as its name. What happened was that one of the other Auditors decided it hadn't been painted in a long time, and here was one of the kids lying around doing nothing, so they hired a couple of these third-generation Allen kids and they painted the bridge. All summer long they painted it. Leaving (and I mean this literally) a trail of green paint on the road all the way from Highway 30 at the Flea Market Corner to the Helen Howe Bridge.

They'd be lying there in the shade under the bridge, humming and going on and sort of waving a paintbrush at the flies, and one of them would say "Hey, we're out of beer." So they'd consider this for a while, and like in the funny papers an imaginary light bulb would suddenly glow over the head of Sonny—he's a thinker, that one— and he'd say "Maybe we'd better go get some more paint." They'd break out a chuckling at that, and leap into the truck and race into Newfane. And cans of green paint kept falling off the back of the truck.

Let us now consider the Vital Statistics on Page 20. Note those ringing Yankee names: Szathmary, Gazeppo, Frankovitch. Obviously stalwart sons of those embattled farmers who stood near that famous rude bridge and fired the shot heard 'round the world.

Back to the Vital Statistics (page 20). Something

scary is happening to our birth rate! In 1972, six children (including four girls, half of them named Kimberly) came to gladden our hearts with colic, diarrhea, and diaper rash. In 1973, however, half this number, or only three children, were born to Brookline mothers. Observers were baffled. Is it the Pill? Low libido? Vermont inscrutability?

Be, however, of good cheer. An unimpeachable source, to wit, Flo Terrill, Town Clerk, Town Treasurer, seller of dog and hunting licenses and general Mother Superior of the West River Valley, reports that as of January 15, 1974, there are no less than five young ladies of Brookline with Something in the oven. And if the Energy Shortage puts an end to (a) snowmobiles, (b) spur-of-the-moment trips to the drugstore in Brattleboro, and (c) watching TV late in warm houses rather than hitting for the blankets early, I have every confidence that by next Spring these hills will echo again with the sweet retching of Morning Sickness.

I thought you might appreciate this guided tour of the Town Report, Mr. Drayton, since you will be soon getting a tax bill indicating Brookline's love and concern. As one of the Town officials, I send it to you out of the traditional concern we all feel for service to people from Outside who live in Connecticut and come up here on weekends to throw beer bottles in our ditches and complain about other people who live in Connecticut and come up here weekends, etc. etc. As a taxpayer, I know you will understand and appreciate our Town Motto, which is, "It Serves You Right."

Cordially,
F. Eugene Godt, Town Auditor

A Deathbed Conversion

The late Father John Mahoney was a brother-in-law of Judge Bernard Leddy, and it's unclear who was the more rabid Democrat. Father Mahoney went with the National Guard as their chaplain in 1941 and on to the South Pacific. When the cruiser *Coolidge* was sunk in 1942, and he was floating in the water with the rest of the troops, he promised Saint Jude that if he were rescued he would build a church in his honor. All but a few *were* rescued. Father John went on to further heroic service, but when the war was over and he was assigned a parish in Hinesburg, he kept his promise to Saint Jude by overseeing a new parish named for the saint.

During his ministry there, he was called to give the last rites to a dying man who lived in the hills northeast of the village. As Mahoney was finishing the anointing, a neighbor stopped to visit. Seeing a priest there, the visitor voiced amazement. "I never knew so-and-so was a Catholic. He's been a Republican all his life!"

Putting the stole and holy oils back into his pocket, Mahoney spoke as if he had brought a sinner forgiveness in the nick of time: "Well, he's a Democrat now!"

☆☆☆☆ GUEST APPEARANCE ☆☆☆☆

Salmonspeak
Tom Slayton

Winston Churchill, it is said, recruited the English language and sent it to war. Many other politicians, less happily, have carpet-bombed its rhythms, sense, and meaning into smoking ruins.

One such warrior was former Vermont governor Thomas P. Salmon. In 1976, after covering the governor for almost four years, Rutland Herald *reporter Tom Slayton wrote an article about Governor Salmon's distinctive idiom, an edited version of which appears here.*

Is a man who finds four legs on a tripod wrong—or is he a prophet?

It probably depends upon your point of view, and this year it might have something to do with your political party.

Simply let it be said that Vermont Governor Thomas P. Salmon has more than a way with the English language; he has many ways. . . . He uses the English language the way a jazz musician uses the chromatic scale.

Salmon's speaking style on the campaign (he was running against U.S. Senator Robert T. Stafford) is far from wooden and pompous. Salmon is possessed of a certain charisma and knows it. In the white-lightning adrenaline rush of pillaging the electorate, the governor comes off very well. He leaves people dazed in his wake, resplendent with the feeling they have somehow had a brush with greatness.

There can be no denying the governor's pure inventiveness. It appears to be a skill he has nurtured thoughtfully over a long period of time, and it employs a variety of modes.

40

At press conferences early in his term, when he wanted to express his intention of looking at all sides of a situation, he would promise to "cover the waterfront" on that question.

Later, when the governor became fond of the word *cosmic*, he would talk about taking a "cosmic overview of the waterfront."

He loved to use the word *summit*. Whenever he had an important meeting with visitors from out of state, it was a "summit conference." Then there were "mini-summits," and once, to discuss migrant problems with apple picking, there was "an apple mini-summit."

Salmon's gubernatorial terms were bedeviled by some of the worst economic times since the Depression. As the state's fiscal crisis grew, so Salmon's figurative language took on darker overtones. He talked a lot about "bottom-line decisions." The people who had to make these decisions usually wore black hats; that is, they had to make unpopular decisions and therefore could not wear white hats like the good guys in the cowboy movies.

Defending his administration's occasionally stern budget-cutting, he observed: "You can't run an army without black hats."

Describing another painful budget process, he said "We have spent six weeks in the agony and ecstasy of wherefore-art-thou revenues to breach this gap."

Describing his loyal opposition, Salmon once said, "When push comes to shove, the Republican party chose to fill the breach with windfalls."

Speaking of breaches, the governor once remarked that a future decision was "one of those brooks too broad for leaping which we have not crossed."

Salmon believed in toughness. When the Public Service Board chairman, Martin Miller, was being battered by public criticism, Salmon came to his defense. He said that Miller "has the mental capacity and emotional stability required to hang tough in the kitchen."

Showing that he had read his Hunter Thompson, Salmon once described public resistance to a strong statewide land-use plan this way: "Land Use is an incendiary word that arouses fear and loathing in the hearts of our people."

Probably his most famous one-liner came during a press conference when he was describing the importance to the state of the University of Vermont and the state colleges. The governor pointed out the influence of manufacturing, tourism, and agriculture, then said "Education is the fourth leg of the tripod of the state's economy."

Showing he knew geometry as well as politics, Salmon once observed: "Everything must be foursquare—if it weren't, it would be lopsided."

In the darkest days of the 1974–75 budget crisis, Salmon prepared the public for further budget cuts with the following: "Unless we seek to perform surgery on this patient now, like ships in the night, we'll be out of town."

But there were moments of hope as well. Salmon reminded his constituents that "the governor can tread on some territory where some angels fear to tread and take the bull by the horns and solve this problem."

At the same time, he promised to exercise caution: "My style is certainly anathema to using the full, ultimate authority of this office."

Salmon could be incisive: "I try to avoid the complete laundry list, litany, cover-the-waterfront approach that some governors feel are necessary."

Even in the darkest days, the governor remained optimistic about the government's ability to solve its various problems: "There are a lot of variety of stratagems." And later: "Since I tend to be somewhat outspoken and on the sunny side of brutally frank, let me say this: Happiness will be level funding."

As the governor girds himself for the political fights to come, we have time to assess the little things about him now. Not the big things, like the way he ran the state. That will come later.

But in the interim, and before the political wars start in earnest, we are free to savor the nuances of our governor's mannerism. This sport has traditionally been a privilege of the governed.

We can recall with glee the number of times Salmon asked us: "How high is up?" in response to a tough question.

As the phrases fade, however, and as the arrows go back forever into their quivers, as the political popularists are shuffled off to Valhalla and we reflect soberly on the facts of life, we may ponder the ultimate truth of Governor Salmon's words when he said in a moment of pure brilliant insight:

"Bureaucracy is full of polysyllables."

Mavis Doyle

By most accounts, Mavis Doyle was the best reporter ever to cover the State House. Once when someone told her a politician was angry with her coverage and was ready for battle, she smiled and said, "That's okay with me—I've got barrels of ink." She was fiercely competitive for her constituents, the people of Vermont.

After she died in 1978, the Vermont Press Association created the Mavis Doyle Award to honor the reporter of the year who best exemplified her qualities: "aggressiveness, determination and compassion; a commitment to the profession; a dedication to social justice; and an unwavering belief that journalism should be the conscience of the government and the voice of the people."

Once, a much-awaited report on special education was to be released. The day before its release was due, Doyle, determined to scoop everyone, hid in the Education Department building, broke into the commissioner's office, got the report, and beat everyone with the story, including the commissioner himself. When Howard Coffin, a *Rutland Herald* reporter, chided her for stealing the document, she replied, "I didn't steal it. It belongs to you and all the people of Vermont. Your taxes paid for it."

On another occasion, Doyle betrayed herself. Determined to listen to some Senate Judiciary Committee discussions that were being held behind closed doors,

she hid in an adjoining room. She propped up her chair next to the door and settled in for an earful. A few minutes later, in burst an apoplectic senator—smoke from the chain-smoking Doyle had curled under the door and alerted the committee to her eavesdropping.

Who's Who?

The Legislative Directory (known colloquially as "the stud book") is the collection of photographs and capsule biographies of all legislators, issued by the secretary of state's office. It makes good reading during dull debates.

During one such floor debate in 1978, Representative Edward Seager of Rutland was thumbing through the book when he paused and flipped back the page. He rose from his seat, walked over to House Clerk Robert Picher, and said, "You know, Edgar May and Madeleine Kunin have something in common—they were both born in Switzerland."

"I'm not surprised," said Picher, swallowing a chuckle. "They *are* brother and sister."

Balding but Unbowed

Kidding men about their growing baldness is a parlor game for some uncharitable souls. Usually, the victims must suffer in silence. Two politicians, however, struck back.

Former governor F. Ray Keyser, Jr., replied to one of the innumerable jibes: "Those who are getting bald around the temples are great thinkers; those who are balding on the top are great lovers; and those who are balding all over *think* they are great lovers."

And Representative William Talbott (D-Monkton) shot back at one tormentor: "The grass does not grow on a busy street!"

Protective Ignorance

In 1986, shortly after U.S. Senator Patrick Leahy's landslide reelection victory, a *New York Times* reporter headed north to interview the future chairman of the Senate Agriculture Committee.

The reporter had vague directions for getting to Leahy's house in Middlesex, and he assumed the neighbors would help him if he got lost.

No such luck.

The following exchange on a Middlesex dirt road took place between the reporter and one of Leahy's neighbors:

"Senator Leahy live up this way?"

"You a relative?"

"No."

"A friend of his?"

"No."

"He expecting you?"

"No."

"Never heard of him!"

Kissinger and Foreign Policy

In the summer of 1976, economist John Kenneth Galbraith hosted a convocation of government leaders and academics at his summer home in Townshend. Out of the gathering came an episode in the BBC series *The Age of Uncertainty*, which Galbraith narrated.

Among the guests was Secretary of State Henry Kissinger.

Before and during those weekend sessions, the Secret Service had its work cut out for it. The unsmiling, wary men had never had to protect public figures in the woods before. So they recruited some local Windham County deputies to help out on the perimeters and to stay with individual guests.

One of those deputies was assigned to walk and ride "shotgun" with Kissinger. After a day and a half of this duty, the deputy had lost some of his awe at his new position, and he felt rather comfortable with the secretary.

On Sunday, Kissinger was driven to the Four Columns Restaurant in Townshend to have lunch. Upon his arrival at the Four Columns, a State Department aide met Kissinger with the day's cables of world events.

As he leafed through the telegrams, he remarked to the aide, "Ach, more shooting in Lebanon."

"Oh, don't worry, Mr. Secretary," interjected the deputy sheriff. "That's over in New Hampshire. It's out of our jurisdiction."

"You can never be sure who they are neutral against."

"We have a many-fauceted problem."

When a new parking garage was dedicated in downtown Rutland: "I want to welcome you all here to see this reality become a supposed dream."

Recounting his wartime service, he told listeners that his troop ship sailed into the Italian "Bay of Maples" and that later he had served on the "Yukoslobovian border."

"You three guys make a pair!"

"Foilage and ski-ism is part of tourism."

"The polls don't count. What counts is what happens when the voters go behind that iron curtain."

"I don't run my campaigns on promises, and I don't build bridges where there ain't no water."

"The business of business is business."

"I like a Republican with no personality over a Democrat with the gift of gab."

"You can lead a horse to water, but you can't look him in the eye."

"That's a horse of a different ballgame."

"We'll burn that bridge when we get to it!"

Nighttime Antics

Back in the days when the Pavilion in Montpelier was a hotel and not a state office building, many politicians stayed there during the weeks when the legislature sat.

One night, Senator T. Garry Buckley (R-Bennington) pulled into the hotel at about two o'clock in the morning. The clerk told him there were no spare rooms, only those reserved by legislators who had not yet arrived. Among those was one for a woman legislator who was due in the next day. Buckley could have that one, the clerk said. He took it.

Now Buckley had a devilish streak in him, and he decided to play a trick on the senator who occupied the adjoining room.

So as soon as he got settled in his temporary room, Buckley began to scratch on the wall. In a few minutes there was some return tapping. This dialogue continued for a few minutes. Then it stopped.

A few minutes later, Buckley heard a sudden knock at the door. He opened it to find the senator arrayed in a dressing gown, shaved, pomaded, and . . . completely embarrassed to see Buckley.

Buckley gave him no quarter—"You've got no business wandering around at this hour! I could have had the house police up here in a moment!" The other senator choked out a few words about suspicious noises, then stumbled back to his own room.

Straight from the Horse's Mouth

Ever-longer legislative sessions were a hallmark of the 1980s. In May of 1982, one Peter Allendorf observed in a letter to *The Burlington Free Press*:

"The recent picture of the sleeping legislator, obviously on 'the peoples' time,' not his own, seems to sum up the general accomplishments of the last gathering of those dedicated public servants.

"Leaderless, they fumbled and bumbled along to one of the longest sessions in modern history. Many old-time residents have indicated to me that in their opinion it was the worst session in state history.

"One, a historian of some experience, told me that many ancient cultures actually elected animals to represent them—the Romans, for example, on occasion elected horses. How fortunate were the Roman citizens; at least they were represented by the entire horse!"

Later, Allendorf himself went on to serve two terms in the Vermont House.

First Things First

Representative Hyacinth Beaulieau (R-Highgate) joined a half dozen Vermont legislators on a trip to Idaho for a conference with the American Legislative Exchange Council. At these retreats, legislators from around the country gather to discuss issues and legislation.

During a break in one session, which took place around the hotel pool, Beaulieau excused himself—he had promised to call home to check in.

When he returned to the group, he reported that things were not only fine, they were festive back at the family farm in Highgate. "It is quite a party—kegs of beer, barbecue, dozens of guests, cousins, aunts, uncles, dancing, the works."

"Gracious, Hyacinth, what are you missing?" asked Representative Barbara Grimes (D-Burlington).

"My fortieth wedding anniversary!"

Of Growth and Girth

In 1988, House Speaker Ralph Wright formed a new committee to deal with the so-called "growth" issue: the House Committee on Growth and Vermont's Future. This new committee was hard put to find meeting space in the already crowded State House. Finally, they lit upon Room 10, one of the two main public meeting rooms. Just as they were settling into the business of the day, Secretary of State James Douglas happened to poke his head in the door. Committee chairman Paul Poirier (D-Barre) at first didn't recognize Douglas, who had shed more than sixty pounds during the previous year. Then he said, "You probably want to be next door."

"How do you know I don't want to be here?" asked Douglas.

"This is about growth, and you've shrunk!" said Poirier.

A Touch of Revenge?

During the 1987–88 session, Speaker Ralph Wright put ten Republicans on the eleven-member Municipal Corporations and Elections Committee. When they complained, he denied he had banished them to obscurity.

The Republicans didn't quite see it that way. They said "Muni Corps" was a backwater of insignificance, and they accused the Speaker of trying to keep them out of the action.

To make their point crystal clear, they hung a sign on the committee room door. Referring to the Mediterranean island to which Napoleon Bonaparte was exiled in 1814, the sign read "Isle of Elba."

P R O C E S S

In the House Ways and Means Committee room, Vern was cleaning out wastebaskets. A snowstorm was forecast outside, but even a big one wouldn't match the blizzard of paper produced by the legislators in the middle of the legislative session inside. He looked around and saw that the piles on the desks were growing higher by the day. Sooner or later, most of that paper would end up in the wastebaskets—for him to dispose of. Some of the desks were pin-neat, but others looked like tornado debris.

In truth, though, the paper was not the biggest annoyance for Vern—that would get recycled. What bugged him most were the candy wrappers, the popcorn, the gum, and the spilled colas and coffee. Those legislators on the Natural Resources Committee, supposedly the environmentalists—they were the biggest slobs of all.

But the most unusual legislative habit was eating candy. Every committee room had some container for gumballs, kisses, mints, and the like. Maybe the candy was a substitute for the now-banned cigarettes. Whatever the cause, most legislators seemed to have an occupational sweet tooth. He dared not speculate on the condition of their teeth.

Tomorrow was the so-called "cross-over day"—the day when bills in each house had to be ready for floor action, if the other body was obliged to consider them before adjournment. Some of the committees were working late, but Ways and Means had departed, since it had an exemption for all money bills.

Outside, snow began to fall through a gray sky that blended with the gray granite state buildings across the street. Inside, on one wall, was a photograph of a Vermont farmer, clad in denims and a battered hat, leaning on a rake. On another wall was a brightly colored painting entitled "Sunset," which to Vern looked more like a bombed-out paint factory.

Chet poked his head in the door. He had been delivering notes to legislators. Usually, he took on that duty after the pages were gone for the day. He didn't mind.

"Try to get done early tonight. They're talking about six to ten inches of snow by morning," he advised.

"Cleaning up after these people takes more time than in most offices. I don't understand how they can be so messy."

"Well, you know, Vern—some of that paper they can't avoid. It comes with the territory. When they try to rewrite bills to make them better, or when they take more testimony, naturally they need paper to convey that information. You can't get away from that in this age."

"Have they ever thought of making fewer laws? Some of these people think their only reason for being is to sit up here and pass bills. They never have to suffer any of the consequences," moaned Vern.

"Making and changing laws is complicated. And there's so much jargon flung around here that sometimes it sounds like people are speaking another language. Over in the Commerce Committee, they flash a sign that reads *Jargon Alert* at witnesses who use too much jargon. It never fails to throw a witness off stride."

"You know what else throws people off? Notes," said Vern. "Legislators practically live by passing notes. They use notes to tell jokes, make snide remarks about other legislators, and even discuss the legislation at hand! I see hundreds of those notes in the wastebaskets on the House and Senate floor."

"Yeah, I saw some of them in your box downstairs."

"You what?!"

Chet reddened. "Oh—I meant I saw some of them when we were down in the basement."

"You're a miserable liar, Chet! You went down and dug through my stories when I asked you not to!"

"I confess. I couldn't resist. Curiosity got the better of me. But I only did it to see what you have. And, Vern, it's quite a stash. You've got the makings of a book there."

Vern looked hurt. "I don't know whether I'm mad or grateful. Guess I'm both."

"Well, I don't blame you for being mad," said Chet. "I knew you were reluctant to share this stuff. But I figured I'd sneak a look at it, and if it was terrible, I wouldn't say anything more. But it isn't terrible. And new stuff keeps coming in. Like someone once said, there are two things you should never watch being made—legislation and pork sausage. And he was right. It's a messy process."

"I agree with that," added Vern, pulling a crumpled card from his pocket. "Listen to this:

> In reporting a Ways and Means Committee discussion of a possible state takeover of the Barre-Montpelier Railroad, Representative Glendon King of Northfield told the House: 'We took this bill up informally in committee and the vote was overwhelmingly un-unanimous!'"

Chet chuckled. "Just keep 'em coming, Vern, and if you ever want my help rewriting, I'm available."

Explaining One's Vote

Legislators sometimes feel called upon to explain their votes, especially when they cross the folks back home. Votes on big money bills like the budget also ignite profuse legislative apologias. Such was the case as the 1991 budget bill came before the House. To balance that budget, the Appropriations Committee had "borrowed"—or "stolen," depending upon one's perspective—sixteen million dollars from the state employees' and teachers' retirement funds.

One of those employees was Representative Herbert O'Brien (R-Stowe). He voted against the budget because: "I have always opposed robbing Peter to pay Paul, but more so when Peter happens to be Herbert J. O'Brien."

Critics especially condemned the merging of multiple elements into a single appropriations bill as a grab-all, a "Christmas tree."

Representative Robert Kinsey (R-Craftsbury), a member of the Appropriations Committee, swallowed his skepticism and voted yes, "even though this is the weirdest Christmas tree I've ever seen. There are some Balm of Gilead leaves that go a Fir piece. It Maple us together and Spruce up state government. However, it has a Slippery Elm trunk. We have added some Weeping Willow branches and some Hardhack taproots. The voters may Cedar differences, but I don't think the Dogwood. Maybe Ole Hickory in the other body will turn it to Ash."

First Things First

Senator Jeb Spaulding (D-Washington) was a part-time stock-raiser and the Education Committee chairman. One day, just before a committee hearing, he was suddenly called home to help search for a prize calf that had escaped from the pasture.

When it came time to open the hearing, Senator Bob Bloomer (R-Rutland) noted the chairman's absence and inquired of the others.

Came the reply from Senator John McClaughry, "I'm afraid Jeb has been de-calfinated."

Earth-Shaking
Decisions at a Selectmen's Meeting

One night in 1982, the Springfield Board of Selectmen was meeting in the town offices.

As the debate heated up, Selectman Bernie Lasuka said "I would like to make a motion." At that moment, the room began to shake. The windows rattled. The lights flickered.

The whole thing lasted only a few seconds, but everyone was a bit unnerved. Chairman V. Joyce Lindamood, however, didn't miss a beat. "If that's the kind of motion you want to make, then you're out of order."

The next day, the newspaper headline read "It's a 4.8-er!" There *had* been a genuine earthquake over in the Adirondacks.

Protecting Wildlife, Real and Imagined

The late Lloyd Selby (R-Derby) once recalled that in the early 1980s Representative Millie Small (R-Hartford) introduced HR 19, a resolution to "protect the so-called Lake Champlain Monster, 'Champ,' or any other mythical things that might be imagined or found."

"I thought this was a rather silly motion," said Selby, "so I got the attention of Speaker Stephen Morse, and when I had the floor, I asked Newport's representatives, William Farrell and Frank Spates, if they thought they were doing their duty in not having some document or resolution passed to protect the fur-bearing fish of Lake Memphramagog.

"I pointed out there was more evidence of the fur-bearing fish than there was of Champ. After all, a mounted specimen of the fur-bearing fish hung in the sergeant-at-arms' office in the State House, but there's not much to prove Champ exists.

"Frank Spates was not about to take this ribbing sitting down. He rose and said:

"'Mr. Speaker, I did see the fur-bearing fish once. I was fishing with my father-in-law from a boat on Lake Memphremagog when the fish appeared. I took another swig from my bottle, and the fish disappeared. I haven't seen one since.'

"Nothing was done at that time nor since, to my knowledge, to protect the poor fish. But the Champ resolution was passed, and it's still on the books for posterity to see how the legislature acts at times with great intelligence."

Lawyers and Lawyers

During the debate on the 1977 appropriations bill, Representative Mary Barbara Maher of South Burlington offered an amendment defining what emergencies the Joint Fiscal Committee could consider when the legislature was not in session. Representative Peter Giuliani of Montpelier, a lawyer, spoke at convoluted length against the amendment, to which she replied, "I'm glad I didn't go to law school and learn all those big words with which to surround by confusing clouds a clear and sunny amendment."

Giuliani (who had clerked to prepare for and pass the bar) replied, "I want to assure the member from South Burlington that I didn't go to law school—and sometimes it shows!"

Two years later, a bill was introduced to require that state's attorneys be lawyers licensed to practice law in Vermont. Giuliani weighed in against the bill: "We should leave the decision of who will be the state's attorney up to the voters. Personally, I trust the good judgment of the voters—even when they vote for me."

Hobbies and Professions

The scene was the House Agriculture Committee room. The time was the late 1960s. The bill under discussion proposed curbs on manure spreading. The committee was seated around a table, with the witnesses in chairs along the wall.

Among the witnesses was a young woman who was earnestly representing the environmental perspective. Dressed in a very short skirt, she spent much of the long meeting trying to stretch her skirt toward her very exposed knees.

After an hour or so of her discomfited squiggling, a bald-headed committee member leaned over to her and, in a stage whisper, said, "Don't worry, miss. My hobby is politics!"

Making Witnesses Ill at Ease

Tired of witnesses who either overqualified their statements or failed to answer direct questions, three members of the House Ways and Means Committee struck back. Representatives Barbara Grimes, Don Hooper, and Mark MacDonald devised and printed a Witness Evaluation List and hung it in the committee room. Witnesses could not fail to read its Dantesque gradations as they faced chairman Oreste Valsangiacomo.

Witness Evaluation List

a. Scrupulously honest
b. Decently accurate
c. An inadvertent omission
d. Hmmm, a slip here or there
e. Disrespectful of the facts
f. Sleight of mouth
g. Verisimilitudinous is too kind
h. Prevaricated
i. A sleazy rip-off
j. The dog ate my testimony

An Admission of Ignorance

During a 1986 debate on why the House Appropriations Committee had cut some money for snowmobile trails, the committee member responsible for that part of the budget, Representative Robert Stannard (R-Manchester), was ill-prepared and stumbled through his explanation.

"Mr. Speaker," he said finally, "I've had about nine minutes to research this. If I may, I would like to yield to the member from Fair Haven, Mr. Wilson, who will tell you everything I don't know."

The Speaker recognized Albert Wilson, vice-chairman of the House Transportation Committee.

"Mr. Speaker," said Wilson, looking at Stannard, "I don't have that much time."

Beauty and the Beholder

The Senate was considering a bill to allocate 1 percent of the construction costs of new state buildings for the purchase of art to be displayed in those buildings.

Senator Francis Howrigan (D-Franklin) is a man of few words, and some of those are acerbic. "What about that scrap iron on the lawn at the University of Vermont?" he asked Senator Robert Gannett (R-Windham). "Will this bill buy more of that?"

"Yes," said the gentle Gannett, "some of that money might buy more art of this sort. You know, Senator, beauty is in the eye of the beholder."

"Yup," grunted Howrigan. "That's what worries me!"

Hugh Moffett

In the mid-1970s, former journalist and Brandon resident Hugh Moffett represented his town in the legislature. He became famous for his one-liners. Once, describing how remote Brandon was, he said there was a local rumor that a fellow had died on the post office steps and hadn't been found for four days.

In 1975, after an interminable debate on a hearing-aid bill, Moffett observed: "Mr. Speaker, I have a terrible hearing problem—I heard every bit of this long debate."

Late in the same session, a resolution was introduced requiring the Department of Education to release the most recent and presumably most accurate data on state aid to education.

Noting that its lateness made the information next to useless in calculating state aid amounts, Moffett rose in opposition:

"Mr. Speaker, I am speaking against this resolution—sort of. At best, this is an exercise in futility. I think we should dispose of the resolution and get on with our other exercises in futility."

Of Duty and Dozing

For seven long hours one April day, the state Environmental Board heard testimony on a land-use permit appeal regarding a proposed hotel on a height of land in Colchester. By three o'clock, yawns were audible.

As witnesses marched to the stand, as the documents and maps piled up on the tables, the board members drifted off to sleep, one by one.

When the final gavel fell, Colchester town manager David Timmons shook his head and sighed. "What do *Roberts' Rules of Order* say about your quorum falling asleep?"

☆ ☆ ☆ ☆ GUEST APPEARANCE ☆ ☆ ☆ ☆

Legislative Survival Kit*
The Rutland Herald

Thursday is the day the Vermont Legislature officially opens, but today is the day the thoughts of legislators turn to packing.

Like summer camp, when Mom made sure you weren't heading for the hills without your toothbrush, lawmakers need to pay close heed to what they pack in their legislative survival kits: their lives could depend on it. There can be looming things and crawly things in the Montpelier State House at this time of year, dark surprises of many kinds, and no legislator is safe without a few basics:

A Blind-Side Shield: A friendly seatmate to the immediate right or left who can provide an early warning when an opponent is sneaking up on a pet bill from the rear. Legislators without friendly seatmates are like sheep without sheepdogs.

A Disciplined Tongue: One that knows when to wag and when to be still. A tongue wagging without wisdom is like a tiger hunting without teeth.

A Padded Seat Cushion: The only thing worse than sitting through a five-hour deer herd hearing is sitting through a five-hour deer herd hearing on a metal chair.

Fair-Mindedness: Fair-mindedness is what happens when a legislator tells another legislator that he plans to vote for him for House Speaker and does. Sleaze is what happens when a legislator says he will vote for one candidate for House Speaker and then votes for someone else because it's done by secret ballot.

*Editorial from *The Rutland Herald*, January 1985

Courage: The ability to say 'no' when everybody else is saying 'yes' when you believe 'no' is the right answer.

Extra Kidney: Handy for budget hearings and long bus rides to Montreal hockey games financed by the beer lobby.

Facts: A rare commodity, especially during deer herd debates.

Thick Skin: Especially useful when the press has just plastered your big mistake all over the front page.

Letting Sleeping Dogs Lie

In 1988, the Vermont House spent three days debating the growth bill. If one defines the importance of a bill as the amount of time spent debating it, the second most important bill the House considered that year may have been the one to curb "dangerous dogs." For five hours the House discussed what was, depending upon one's outlook, either a necessary law to protect the public from a new class of four-legged villains—that is, pit bulls and their ilk—*or* the overturning of a long Vermont tradition of giving dogs their so-called "one free bite."

Some members took the debate lightly and titters were audible. But the bill's sponsor, Representative Ralph Baker (R-Randolph), was all seriousness as he delivered his report on the floor of the House.

When he finished, the questions began. The bill used the word *worrying* to refer to the dogs' behavior; could another, more specific word be used? asked one member. Baker said *worry* came from a Greek root meaning "snapping or tearing at." "It *has* a specific legal meaning," he said.

Is "repetitious behavior" the mark of a dangerous and irresponsible dog? asked another member.

"This bill is about both irresponsible dogs and irresponsible owners," Baker shot back pug-naciously.

"Well, it would put real teeth in the dog laws," observed one member.

"The previous speaker is right. This is no bare-bones bill," seconded another representative.

Would the bill cover "junkyard dogs"—those left in a junkyard to protect the premises against intruders? asked one member.

"Yes," replied Baker.

"That's good," sighed the other. "One of 'em once got me. He broke his chain and bit me, but fortunately, it didn't hurt much—caught me in the wallet."

The original bill, which had been written in conjunction with the Humane Society, called for every such dog to be tattooed with a designation of *dangerous dog,* but that was stricken when it was discovered there were no tattoo parlors in Vermont. Instead, the bill required that the owner securely attach to the dog's collar a steel stamp with the words *dangerous dog* embossed thereon.

Several representatives remarked that by the time one got close enough to read the stamp, it would be too late.

By then, it was clear the bill had problems. One representative suggested it be sent back to the "kennel—er, committee."

"My head is bloodied but un-bow-wowed," sighed Baker.

At the Speaker's direction to rephrase the motion, the member did request and the body agreed to "order the bill to lie."

(As it turned out, the bill was brought up again. It passed the House, but it died in the Senate for lack of time at the end of the session.)

Out You Go

Robert Kinsey (R-Craftsbury) tells the following story.

"When I was House majority leader [1981–85] and assistant majority leader [1977–81], I always felt that my prime responsibility was to those who had elected me to that position—the Republican Caucus.

"Governor Richard Snelling was a strong and forceful leader, and most intelligent. Our caucus backed him on most of his issues. There were a few issues, however, that didn't receive our caucus's support. Most notable of these were the statewide property tax, decoupling from the federal income tax structure, and the repeal of the ninety-percent bonding rule. (This latter required the state to bond for no more than ninety percent of the amount of bonds that would be retired that year.)

"Once a week or so, the three Republican leaders of the House and their counterparts from the Senate met with the governor in his State House office. On one occasion, the governor gave a scholarly lecture on the need to repeal the ninety-percent rule. He was aware that I was the only one of the six who needed the lecture. To further impress me, he pointed his finger at each of the leaders, leaving me for last.

"'Stew [Smith] are you with me?' 'Yes.' 'Bob [Bloomer]?' 'Yes.' 'Bob [Gannett]?' 'Yes.' 'Steve [Morse]?' 'Yes.' 'Susan [Auld]?' 'Yes.' 'Kinsey?'

"'No.'

"There were deep breaths all around. Then came scholarly lecture number two. My response was, 'Well, Governor, we have some other issues to discuss.'

"So we did and there was agreement on these.

"Then the governor came back to the ninety-percent rule. 'So, Bob, are you with me?'

"Again I said no, feeling my responsibility to my Republican Caucus.

"Lecture number three was not as pleasant or as scholarly.

"'Well, young man'—Snelling is my senior by six months—'we're going to run right over you. We will run a candidate against you in Craftsbury, and you won't be coming back.'

"I said, 'You are most welcome to do that.'

"Aware that the governor might push hard on the ninety-percent rule repeal, I had polled the House members. I continued: 'As for the repeal, I have in my pocket a roll call sheet with one hundred and eight members voting no.'

"Governor Snelling rose to his feet, slammed both fists on the table, and left the room.

"Speaker Steve Morse observed, 'Bob, I've seen the governor kick other people out of his office, but this is the first time I ever saw him kick himself out!'"

Praying to the Fullest

Each morning the Vermont Senate and House open with prayers and a short homily delivered by guest clergy. One day the clergyman had the senators on their feet, then seated, then on their feet, then seated again like boot camp recruits. One freshman senator observed that all the up-and-downing gave new meaning to the term *devotional exercises*.

"No," another replied, "they're called prayerobics."

The Big Chill Budget

In 1986, Todd Shapera, a free-lance writer, came to Montpelier to do a story about Vermont's citizen legislature for National Public Radio. To prepare for his interview with Governor Madeleine Kunin, he asked a gubernatorial aide, Marty Hannifin, for a copy of the state budget. Hannifin was a little nervous, but he led Shapera to a small refrigerator in the governor's State House office. There, neatly stacked inside the appliance, were a half dozen copies of the two-hundred-page document.

When Shapera came to interview the governor, he told her about finding the budgets in the refrigerator. Kunin didn't believe him and asked to be shown the new document repository. Sure enough, there they were—right beneath the milk.

Surprised, the governor asked Hannifin why this repository had been chosen.

"It was the only place we could put them and know they'd be safe from the press and legislators until after the budget address," replied Hannifin.

Modern Legislative "Sausage"

A witness before the Senate Natural Resources Committee was explaining how hospitals dispose of discarded medical instruments and syringes through a hammer mill process:

"The 'sharps,' like syringes and scalpels and other metal parts, are put into this hammering device, which rather noisily reduces them to a shapeless lump that can be disposed of."

"We're familiar with that process," interjected Senator John McClaughry (R-Caledonia). "We do that to legislation in this room all the time."

Gender Neutrality Carries the Day

In 1989, the House struck a blow for feminism with a petition to rid itself of the term *chairman*. The proposal came in the form of a poem composed by Representative Ann Seibert (D-Norwich):

The Chair

The chair is a chair
Is a chair, you say,
To sit on and stand on
Or get in the way.

But to head a committee
Use chairman forever.
Chairperson, chairwomen,
Chairpeople—Chair? Never!

Furniture can define us
One way or another,
Not as men or as women
Or as father or mother.

Some issues we table,
We couch our remarks,
The floor can be taken
To spill out our hearts.

Bureaucrats hound us daily
Not Bureau men.
When the Bench is approached
It's not Bench women.

Sweet music from Speakers
Is not always heard.
Speaker man? Speaker woman?
There's no extra word.

Chair alone is environmentally sound,
Printing paper and trash
Would be saved all around.

Representatives, Senators,
Let's clean up our act.
We're in this together,
That is a fact.

To use Chair and Vice Chair,
The ear hears the truth.
Let's try it before
Someone goes through the roof.

The change passed the House Rules Committee and went into effect soon thereafter.

O Tempora! O Mores!

In the spring of 1986, there came to the House floor via the Health and Welfare Committee a Senate bill "relating to the licensing of persons who perform manicures and facials."

Reporting the bill for the committee was Representative Eugene Godt (D-Brookline).

Almost every bill that is introduced in either house includes a few definitions of words that relate specifically to the proposed legislation. So Godt began his report by reading the definition of *esthetics*.

"Mr. Speaker, esthetics means massaging, cleansing, stimulating, exercising, beautifying, or otherwise working on the scalp, face, neck, arms, bust, or upper part of the body, by the use of any manner of cosmetic preparations, antiseptics, tonics, lotions, or creams."

Godt paused. "Now, Mr. Speaker, those are the words of either an inspired poet, or a word processor in heat!"

The House burst into laughter. When that died down, Godt remarked: "Mr. Speaker, I think I have lost my place!"

"I thought you had *found* it, Member from Brookline," observed Speaker Ralph Wright.

"Well," said Godt, "I *have* had two sinking feelings and a hot flash just standing here."

☆☆☆☆ GUEST APPEARANCE ☆☆☆☆

Madeleine's Legislative Dictionary
Madeleine Kunin

In the mid-1970s, when Madeleine Kunin was in the legislature, she wrote up this dictionary of legislative terms with her own definitions.

Housekeeping bill: "This is a simple housekeeping bill" is the best way to provoke both laughter and suspicion. Occasionally, the term does apply to minor technical changes in the law, but often, it is applied to bills which make sweeping changes.

Poorly drafted bill: A favorite euphemism for opposing a bill.

Needs further study: See above.

This bill is unconstitutional: Surprisingly enough, this doesn't impede passage. And sometimes, it helps.

The BIG bill: The Appropriations bill. It IS big.

Fish and game bill: Sit back and relax. The debate will last about two hours.

House rules: Meticulously observed until the final week of the session.

Roll call vote: When you're grateful that your name begins with "W."

Strike-all amendment: Shows that the committee has worked hard and the result may or may not have anything to do with the original bill.

Small grammatical change: Such as changing "may" to "shall" which may [shall] totally change the meaning of the bill.

The other body: Other legislative chamber. Location is usually not discovered until late in the session.

Party discipline: "You are free to vote your conscience, but . . ."

"Point of order": Sure way to make someone opposing your bill stop in the middle of a sentence.

Strategy: When you have asked a few people to speak in favor of your bill: a liberal, a conservative, a Democrat, a Republican, some on the left side of the aisle, some on the right side, the front row, the back rows, and one each from the Northeast Kingdom, Chittenden County, the Banana Belt, the Connecticut River, and Canada.

Count votes: Arithmetic best done before a bill is brought to a vote.

Take a walk: An irresistible urge felt by some legislators to jog around the State House when a controversial roll call is imminent.

Satisfy all your constituents: Vote one way in committee and the opposite way on the floor.

"See if it will fly": Words of encouragement given to a freshman legislator doing something no one in his right mind would dare to do.

A balanced bill: A bill that pleases the Associated Industries of Vermont, the AFL-CIO, Planned Parenthood, Right to Life, Burlington, and Rutland.

"I had not planned to get up and speak on this issue": Introduction to a one-hour speech.

"My people tell me": I got two letters on this subject, one from Aunt Matilda.

"I have polled my district": I called up Aunt Matilda and she wants this bill.

Farmers' night: One night a week when the well of the House becomes a legitimate stage.

Committee Unity: Fight your chairman in the committee room and not on the floor.

Lobbyists: People who oppose your bill.

Citizens: People who support your bill.

Damned with Faint Praise

In Vermont politics, nothing is ever certain.

Yankee obstinacy, independence, and just plain orneriness run deep in the veins of these granite hills. Nowhere is that fact more easily observed than at town meeting.

To wit: During a town meeting in a small town north of St. Johnsbury during the 1970s, there appeared on the warning the following article:

"Resolved that the town extend to Judson Tucker and his family its condolences on the loss by fire of their barn, car, and toolshed."

The following vote was duly recorded in the minutes:
Aye 121
Nay 102

John McClaughry tells the following story of his first town meeting as moderator.

"I'm from southern Illinois originally. At my second town meeting in Kirby I was elected moderator of the town meeting. (This was a fluke—I was the only candidate present.) I was very surprised and nervous but managed to stumble through the morning session. In line for lunch my confidence was swelled immensely when I overheard a review of my performance spoken in an approving tone: 'Ain't from around here, but he's a hick from somewhere.'"

Hard at Work

Vermont, it is suspected, has never really accepted the fact that she gave up nationhood with her entrance into the Union in 1791. Every once in a while, the specter of a Vermont national foreign policy rises above the fog in the State House. A good example of this is the following resolution, passed by the House on March 24, 1977.

Mr. Moffett of Brandon offered a resolution, entitled Resolution Welcoming the Atlantic Islands of Nantucket and Martha's Vineyard;

Whereas, the Atlantic Islands of Nantucket and Martha's Vineyard have declared intention to secede from Massachusetts as a result of deprivation of representation by a state gerrymander, and

Whereas, in pursuance of that intention the islands have created an independent flag and anthem, and

Whereas, the revolting islands have signified an interest in aligning with a state more considerate, especially Vermont, and

Whereas, the state of Vermont, though shown on the map between Lake Champlain and the Connecticut River, is known to have a heart that extends unbounded to the crack of dawn on the east, the Southern Cross to the south, the Evening Star in the west and on the north to the Aurora Borealis, *now therefore be it*

Resolved by the House of Representatives:
That the Vermont House of Representatives offer a refuge to these salty castoffs, *and be it further*

Resolved: That the Governor of Vermont send at once two emissaries to open talks, *and be it further*

Resolved: That said emissaries be one of Republican and one of Democratic persuasion so that their possible entreaties to the inhabitants of the islands do nothing to possibly upset the happily current delicately balanced Democratic majority of the Vermont House, *and be it further*

Resolved: That said emissaries suggest there is no reason the natives of the mountains, the land of milk, honey and syrup, cannot dwell happily forever with the tidal tribes and catchers of the cod.

I S S U E S

It was late May. The legislative session was in its fourth "last week." The end was near. Most of the work was being done by small "Committees of Conference," groups of three members from each body that meet to resolve differences on bills. The rest of the legislators lounged around, reading the newspaper, drinking coffee, socializing, dreaming about the next session, or vowing never to come back. Pessimists talked darkly about going into June. Editorialists called upon the legislature to finish its business. The legislative leaders and the governor, however, proclaimed that "good legislation could not be rushed."

Vern and Chet met for coffee in the big airy State House cafeteria. Around them milled lawmakers. Chet had ten minutes off, then he had to get back to his message-delivering rounds.

Several groups or pairs of people were seated at various tables around the cafeteria. Right in the middle, under a skylight, sat Speaker Ralph Wright and a few of his supporters.

90

"There's the most powerful man in Vermont—at least, he is in these last few days and weeks of the session," said Chet.

"How 'bout the governor?" asked Vern.

"No, the Speaker's the man who controls the flow, who sends his troops out to battle with the enemy senators or administration."

"What flow?" retorted Vern. "The end of the session makes me think of bumper cars at the fair. Some kids work to get their cars through, while others have fun just trying to block them. Nobody really gets anywhere."

"Bumper cars. I like that," said Chet. "Of course the big difference is that in bumper cars there's no cop, unless you count the guy on the switch. Here you have a cop, and he has the biggest car of all—that's Ralph Wright. He's the one who says who gets which car, who gets through the traffic light. He's happy to let people drive fast and bump small cars, but he's running the show.

"Any speaker has that kind of influence in the last days of the session," Chet continued. "And besides, you're forgetting the substance—the causes and issues that put people into those bumper cars in the first place. They aren't out there crashing around at random. They're usually trying to get somewhere."

"Time out!" Vern said suddenly. "This is getting too heavy. We're going to write a *funny* book. Let the reporters write about all that serious stuff."

"You're right," said Chet. "I suppose even in the issues there's humor."

"Sure there is. One day Frank Spates from Newport was about to speak in favor of a bill to allow Sunday shopping. Before he talked about the bill, though, he said: 'I want to assure the members that I believe in God and that I am one of those who wants to put prayers back in the churches.'"

"You got any more like that?"

"Yeah, a bunch."

91

Purple Prose Award

The well of the House is a grand chamber of severe and stately proportions. As the largest room in the State House, it hosts the largest public hearings. Once or twice a year, there is a hearing that fills the chamber with impassioned, curious, angry, committed folks. Underneath the massive bronze chandelier marches a parade of witnesses to praise or denounce seatbelts, gay rights, a doe season, abortion, or what-have-you.

One cold evening in the spring of 1986, a proposed banning of leg-hold traps brought out more than 250 citizens. Speaking in opposition, one Wayne Hurlburt of Chittenden County won the Purple Prose Award when he asserted: "There is a radical sewer that starts in Chittenden County and flows toward Montpelier. Within this system you will find ninety percent of all the professional demonstrators, anti-groups, and troublemakers in the state of Vermont. It was in the contaminated waters of this system that this bill was spawned."

The Great Seat Belt Debate

In 1986, a bill to require the wearing of seat belts came before the full House. For over two days the members debated this "sensible contribution to public safety and welfare" or "this further governmental meddling in the rights of free citizens," depending upon their perspective.

As the debate proceeded, opponents and supporters sought to amend the bill, either to make it more acceptable or to make it more ridiculous and cumbersome. Exemptions were suggested for garbage truck drivers, emergency medical personnel, and delivery workers. Each new amendment was greeted with louder groans. Finally, an exemption for volunteer firemen was suggested. Much serious debate ensued, even though the bill, as written, called for seat belt use only if seat belts were built into the vehicle. There were no seat belts on the back of firetrucks.

Representative Ann Harroun (D-Essex) went out into the lobby for a break and heard a solution for the firemen's dilemma: "Why don't they just put a big strip of Velcro around the trucks and add Velcro to the firemen's coats, and they can just jump on board and hold on that way?"

She returned to the floor just in time to hear a final exemption offered by Representative Keith Wallace (R-Waterbury): "Mr. Speaker, I must ask permission to offer one more exception to this proposed law—for legislators—who are already equipped with air bags!"

Strung Up by His Peers

George Crosby (R-St. Johnsbury) introduced a bill to relieve newspapers of the requirement of paying unemployment compensation to free-lancers, or so-called "stringers." When he appeared before the House Commerce Committee to explain the bill, he asked if the members all knew what a stringer was.

"Shoah, George," drawled Lloyd Selby(R-Derby). "It's the line you drag alongside the boat, holding the catch until you decide which fish to keep."

Let Me Rephrase That . . .

Sometimes politicians can be too clever. During a debate on a snowmobile bill, Representative Jack Candon (D-Norwich) remarked, "In my town of Norwich, people think that a snowmobile is a Volvo with four snow tires." A number of constituents let him know they were not amused. No more amused were the residents of Walden when Lieutenant Governor T. Garry Buckley remarked that "in Walden a seven-course meal is a six-pack of beer and a jacked deer steak."

Other politicians are more clever than they mean to be.

In 1978, a bill was proposed to extend the mandatory closing time for bars on Sunday mornings. Representative Don Ennis (R-Barre Town) was explaining a legislator's point that the closing hours should be left up to the Liquor Control Board. Bars would be free to set their own closing hours at up to three o'clock in the morning.

"Thus, not everyone would leave the bars at the same time," said Ennis. "In other words, it would be possible to *stagger* those leaving the bars."

Hypothetical situations for prospective legislation are posed in ways that are sometimes friendly, sometimes adversarial, and sometimes ambiguous. In 1980, a representative from Rutland Town interrogated a legislator who had reported a bill on fair employment practices this way: "Look, I'm a farmer. I hire men and women to milk my herd. Suppose a woman employee were to get pregnant and get kicked by a cow she was milking. Am I, as her employer, responsible for her condition?"

In the 1989 omnibus transportation bill there was a section to establish a number of "scenic corridors" throughout the state. Cynics called this phrase a euphemism for strip development, while the bill's supporters argued that it would bring more tourist dollars to the respective regions. In any case, several members sought to extend the "scenic corridors" into their own districts.

In reporting this amendment to the whole House, Representative Paul Hannan (R-Holland) contended that the scenic corridor along Route 100 should be extended to Newport to "show that life doesn't stop at Morristown." During subsequent debate he received an anonymous note that agreed: "No, life doesn't stop in Morristown, but it does slow down a good bit!"

In the spring of 1985, the Burlington Board of Aldermen was debating a resolution to declare Burlington a sanctuary for Central American refugees. Proponents said it was a good way to protest Reaganite policies in that war-torn region.

Opponents wondered about the cost, the strains on the schools, the cultural shock, and so forth. Alderman Fred Bailey (R-Ward 6) cautioned, "I'm sure those who come won't have 2.2 kids and an American Express Card."

How to Read the Town Report*
M. Dickey Drysdale

There's more than one way to read through the town report. Here, M. Dickey Drysdale provides an in-depth lesson on how to read it correctly.

"I have to get two copies of the town report," explains an acquaintance, "because I eat the first one alive."

In the Old Days there were lots of people, who, like our friend, really knew how to devour a town report. These days, a lot of folks would like to participate in town affairs, but they haven't quite gotten the hang of it. Since reading the town report is an important first step, we offer these easy rules.

1. Turn first to the list of delinquent property taxes. There is simply no other place to begin, and experienced hands generally spend about half their time on these pages. Depending upon your preconceptions of the people listed, your reactions may range from "Gee, George must've had a tough year" to "That William, he's a scumbucket," to "Wonder why Margaret didn't pay that $7.38. Must be a story there" (and then you try to find it out).

2. Turn next to the vital statistics. Try to determine, using two years of town reports, whether nine months elapsed between the marriages and the births.

3. Turn to the budgets. You spend more time on the town budget, even though the schools spend much more. This is because you understand what hot mix is and how to lay it down, but you're not sure what goes on in school these days.

4. Look at the "bottom line" under expenses, comparing this year's total to last year's. Swear. Then go back

*Reprinted with permission from *Vermont Life*

through the budget, line by line, and find out where the increases were. Circle them in red for a Town Meeting confrontation.

5. Find out what percentage of the budget is under "administration." No matter how low it is, it's too high.

6. Find out how much the town manager earns. In a town like Randolph, with multiple accounts, this is not easy, since parts of the manager's salary are in about six different places. Nevertheless, it is important for the compleat town report reader to find them all and add them up, right down to the penny.

6-A. A new wrinkle. Find out how much money is being spent on computers. This takes a similar search through all the various accounts, since computers are now saving money, and spending it, in every corner of town government.

7. Turn to the tax rate page. No matter what the numbers say, observe to yourself that taxes keep going up and will never stop. If you don't have kids in the school system, notice particularly that the school tax is much bigger than the town tax.

8. A general rule: Read all numbers in the town report before you read any words. Numbers tell you what you want to know; words are just excuses.

9. The written reports can, however, sometimes tell you who is blaming whom for what. So read them. The only things absolutely not worth reading are reports written by public relations specialists, but there aren't many of these. The nice thing about town reports is that real people write them, not writers.

10. Finally, and for extra credit: Find out how much it cost to print the town report. Then make a list of every typographical error in the report, and swear that if you were a selectman you would find a new printer.

Protecting the Neighborhood

In the early 1970s, waves of immigration were still washing over Vermont. To some natives, the "hippie invasion" constituted a threat to public decency, since these newcomers seemed to do a lot of nude swimming in Vermont's streams and ponds.

Several legislators drafted a bill to prohibit this nefarious activity, legislation that became known as the "skinny-dipping bill."

When it reached the House floor, one of the bill's supporters, Representative Robert Emond (D-Brattleboro), spoke on the dangers that would surface if this bill were not passed. He described how much more common lewd and lascivious behavior was already becoming.

"Why, down in Brattleboro," he said, hitting his stride, "it's getting to be that the sex act is becoming natural!"

Who Said Alaska
Has the Biggest Mosquitos?

In 1988, under pressure from mosquito-ridden constituents around Lake Dunmore, Senator Chester Ketcham (R-Addison) introduced a bill to establish a mosquito eradication program under the direction of the Agriculture Department. The bill passed the Senate, but it languished in the House Agriculture Committee until the last week of the session. Then it emerged shorn of its liability insurance component, which led one committee member to remark, "This is the wrong way to get on the right track."

On the last day of the session, the bill reached the floor.

Serious reservations about the bill's implications soon became light-hearted queries. Elmer Faris, a retired farmer who was given to blunt and colorful speech, represented Barnet, which includes the village of "Mosquitoville." Representative Kenyon of Bradford asked to interrogate "the member from Mosquitoville," in the hope that Faris could offer some insight into the problem.

"What would the member from Mosquitoville suggest we do with these insects?" Kenyon asked.

"Member from Bradford, I would suggest—and it's only a suggestion—that for those mosquitos between two-and-a-half and three pounds, you use box traps!"

Representative Langdon Smith (R-New Haven) next pointed out that if passed with the amendments added, the bill would go into effect on September 1, 1988—*after* the mosquito season ended. The Agriculture Department would not report to the legislature until February 1, 1989, during which time few of the pesky insects would be flying. The bill would then sunset on June 30, 1989. "It would seem we are hiring two people for fifty thousand dollars to do nothing!"

"Not nothing," suggested Representative Robert Kinsey (R-Craftsbury). "That's what it costs to mount a S.W.A.T. team!"

A year later, an "aquatic nuisances" bill came to the floor—it too contained references to mosquito control. Representative Kenyon again rose to interrogate Faris: "Mayor of Mosquitoville, since you rule the one municipality in the state where mosquitos and humans live in utmost harmony and concord, what's your opinion of this bill?"

"Mr. Speaker," said the gravel-voiced Faris, "as I read this bill, it doesn't *require* mosquito control. That's good. If it did, we'd be worried. Because, by July first, we like to get 'em up to barbecue size—'bout three pounds—and a mandated program would obviously cut down on the numbers."

Protecting Lobbyists from Exposure

In the waning days of the 1990 session, the House passed a much-toughened lobbyist disclosure bill that would require, among other things, that lobbyists detail all their expenditures above five dollars to influence legislation. Despite stickier going in the Senate, it passed that body and was signed by Governor Kunin.

Representative Merrill Perley (R-Enosburg) recalled that he had introduced the first lobbyists' bill in the Vermont House in 1959. The bill would have merely required lobbyists to pay a five dollar registration fee.

It had been killed, in part, because of the opposition of Representative Margaret Hammond (R-Baltimore), who penned the following doggerel:

I have a few words for you at this time.
So thought I would put them down in a rhyme.

I just couldn't sleep, so I got up early,
To consider this bill, brought in by Perley.

The Committee worked on the bill and its bearings
To shorten the sessions, no waiting for hearings.

We thought all the lobbyists, and many more
Would come to speak on it, but only four

Showed up to tell us all about
Why we the Committee should not re-route

The people from the Capitol's door,
or pay a fee of $5.00 or more.

Corporations, education or religion, should have the right
To come before us day or night.

Political scientists and free men
Should not have to tell us their reason.
Either for or against, or in any season,
The doors of this Assembly should always be open,

To any and all, who wish words to be spoken
So the member from Milton offered to sort
All the material we got and give the adverse report.

Unwanted Federal Aid
John McClaughry

*On February 2, 1989, a U.S. Air Force FB-111A fighter
bomber crashed in Kirby, Vermont, near the New Hampshire border. The pilot and radar navigator ejected safely.
They were discovered by Jeff Eastman and Al Eaton, who
guided the airmen to Eaton's farmhouse. The next day, Air
Force personnel cordoned off the field where the bomber
crashed and collected all pieces of wreckage.*

*A month later, at the Kirby town meeting, moderator
John McClaughry made the following remarks:*

"By now Kirby residents are well aware of the unfortu-
nate crash of an Air Force FB-111 several weeks ago.

"For years, we in Kirby have starved and frozen without any attention from our federal government, which has
been shipping billions hither and yon without so much as
a howdee-do to us.

"Finally, the federal government dropped thirty-three
million dollars in our town, and within twelve hours they
have fifty men up here picking it up and taking it back.
Typical.

"The incident also illustrates the dangerous conditions
at Kirby International Airport.

"While it is possible to land a high-performance jet on
our lone twenty-five-foot runway, as we have just seen, it
is apparently not possible to do so at a glide path angle of
less than about eighty-nine degrees. That does not make
Kirby International very attractive to most pilots.

"By the Selectmen's calculations it will cost about
eighty-five million dollars to correct the situation, or fifteen thousand dollars if all we do is cut the stumps closer
to the ground.

"I want to congratulate Al and Terry Eaton for their hospitality to the downed fliers. When Jeff Eastman brought them to Eaton's farmhouse and one of them growled, 'Boy, I could use a drink right now,' Terry ran and got a glass of sparkling Kirby spring water for him without a second thought.

"Fellow citizens, Kirby has made it through another year, despite the worst the higher levels of government could do to us. As in Periclean Athens, this is once again an occasion to celebrate."

Of Bears, Dogs, and Legislators

Fish and wildlife bills are red meat for both legislative lions and legislative mice. Every member has an opinion on them, yet for very few solons is their vote a matter of political life or death (though the rhetoric can sound dire at times).

In the 1990 session, the winning entry in this category was H-878, "An act relating to hunting bears with dogs." It set controls on the use of dogs when hunting black bears. The amended bill passed the House and the Senate Natural Resources Committee, with one difference. Where the House version read, "No person shall pursue, either for training or taking purposes, black bear with the aid of dogs without a permit issued by the commissioner," the Senate version read, "No person shall pursue black bear with the aid of dogs, either for training or taking purposes, without a permit issued by the commissioner."

When the bill appeared on the Senate calendar for action, it read: "H-878. An act relating to hunting bare with dogs."

Unwilling to let hunting dogs lie, Senator John McClaughry (R-Caledonia) offered four jocular alternative versions on the Senate floor:

Version 1—"No person shall run after a black bear which is being aided by a dog, whether for training or taking purposes, without a permit issued by the commissioner."

Version 2—"No dog, without a permit from the commissioner, shall pursue a black bear on behalf of any person, whether for training or taking purposes, or for no discernible purpose at all."

Version 3—"No person, clothed or bare, shall pursue dogs with the aid of bear and no bear shall pursue persons with the aid of dogs. No dog shall pursue bear with the aid of persons."

Version 4—"No combination of bears, dogs, persons, and commissioners shall pursue any other combination of bears, dogs, persons, and commissioners, without a permit issued by a party not pursuing or being pursued."

Bugged!

During his terms in office, Governor Richard Snelling complained several times that his office was bugged, because some private conversations ended up in the press. Reporters pooh-poohed the idea, and they suggested that the notoriously thin-skinned Snelling was just paranoid.

As it happened, a former page dropped in to the executive offices and, in conversation with Snelling aide James Douglas, asked, "Don't you know about the air shaft up on the third floor?"

"No," said Douglas, "but we'll check it out."

Several days later, Douglas climbed the circular staircase to the third floor of the State House. There he entered a small room which contained a raised platform shielded by a curtain.

Douglas pulled the curtain aside. Behind it he found Louis Berney, a *Rutland Herald* reporter, standing on a table with his ear pressed against the air shaft, which led down to the governor's second-floor office.

Caught dead to rights, Berney said he had only listened a "couple of times."

Within the week, workmen had boarded up the air shaft.

☆ ☆ ☆ ☆ GUEST APPEARANCE ☆ ☆ ☆ ☆

Submarginal Happiness*
George Aiken

During the summer of 1934 a band of emissaries from the Resettlement Administration appeared in the Vermont hills and concentrated their efforts upon securing options looking to the purchase of four large areas of land in somewhat sparsely populated hill sections of southern and central Vermont. The people living in these communities were poor. Many of them owed money in about the same proportion to their wealth that some of their more ostensibly prosperous brethren owed money. Their homes contained few modern conveniences. Some of them lived a considerable distance from school, and much of the land on the farms they occupied was rather stony and in small fields.

The boys sent up from Washington went among these people. They pointed out to them the great degree of unhappiness which they suffered. They painted pictures of the prosperity and great joy which would be theirs should they sell their homes to the Federal government and accept a loan which would set them up in a more regal manner in the lower land of the valleys. When these rural citizens protested that they were not unhappy; that they lived on these poor, rocky farms from choice; that they did not like the idea of going deeper into debt, and furthermore did not intend to move off their farms just because some crack-brained professor thought it would be good for them, then the boys from Washington resorted to other means by which to get options on the land. They told them that if they did not sell to the government, schools and roads in these areas would be given up and they would be left in isolation. And some were convinced that they had to sell and move out whether they wanted to or not.

*From *Speaking from Vermont* by George Aiken. New York: Frederick A. Stokes Company, 1938.

In January, 1935, while this taking of options was in progress, the Vermont Legislature met; and the powers that be, or were, of the Resettlement Administration descended upon Montpelier. Such a display of flattery—attorneys, theorists, scientists, doctors of all degrees—converged upon us. We should have been greatly honored. This was February, and usually Federal officials arrange to do their work in Vermont between June and October.

They placed before the members of the legislature the astonishing story that, not only were these people in certain areas of the State very unhappy because of their condition, but that the State itself was very unhappy because such people existed in such areas. Vermont was very, very sick. It would continue to be sick until fifty-five percent of its area had been transferred to Federal control; and the purchase of over nineteen thousand acres in the four areas selected was but the initial start toward the acquisition of this fifty-five percent. This, of course, would be turned back to the State just as soon as it had all been fixed up in apple-pie order by the Federal government, so as to yield a continuous and enormous profit to the State.

What of the fact that the people in the areas concerned did not care to be moved from their homes? Well, possibly these people weren't of high enough mental capacity to understand that they really were unhappy. A little State and Federal legislation would make them happy whether they wanted to be or not, because the law would henceforth compel them to be.

The Vermont legislators exchanged strange looks on hearing the story from Washington. Some of them indulged in sly grins. Others maintained poker faces. The majority kept tongues in their cheeks. But all listened courteously.

So the Legislature authorized the appointment of a committee to confer with Federal authorities and ascertain if it were advisable to grant them the right to purchase what they were pleased to call submarginal areas. There was a bit of irony in this legislative action, which made your author chairman of the State board. There was a bit of irony in that the legislators knew that he lived on a very submarginal farm. There was a bit more irony in this legislative action in making the Speaker of the House a member of the board, for the legislators knew that the Speaker lived comfortably in an area which was rated as a hundred percent submarginal for twenty miles in all directions from his home.

The committee then asked upon what terms the land would be turned back to the State. Federal hands were thrown in the air in horror. Why, the very idea! No other State in the Union had even asked to know upon what terms this land would be returned to them. They all trusted their Uncle Sam. They knew that whatever terms were submitted would, of course, be to the advantage of the States, with Uncle playing the role of benefactor. One glorious recreational area would be provided for the State. Three wonderful forest areas. Miles of road would be abandoned, relieving the State and towns of the necessity of keeping them repaired. Schools could be abandoned, saving more expense. Why did we have to know the terms upon which this land would be returned to the State? Federal eyes wept with sadness to think that Vermont should even want to know the terms. But the Vermont committee, surrounded by submarginal land which had supported generation after generation, was adamant. We would either know the terms that the Federal government proposed to make in this matter, or there would be no sale.

Back to Washington went messengers, and Federal attorneys scratched their heads and forthwith wrote out a contract which we were assured would be to the everlasting benefit of Vermont. The contract provided that the Federal government should purchase the land in Vermont, pay for it out of Federal funds, develop it with Federal funds, and then turn it back to the State on a long-time lease. In turning it back to the State, the Federal government would incidentally retain ownership of all oils, minerals and similar natural products. All the State had to do to take advantage of the munificent offer was to agree that it would maintain and operate these areas in such manner as the Federal authorities might direct and pay the expenses of maintenance forever. And also that we would never again permit any of this land to be occupied as homes.

The Federal government did not buy any submarginal land in Vermont.

Bringing Home the Bacon

In 1982, a developer in Stowe sought to place a motel in the last large open meadow on the Mountain Road. He was turned down because it was said the land ought to be used for farming. "All right," said the developer, and, in retaliation, he proposed to build a pig farm on the property.

In one of Bill Mares's radio editorials on South Burlington station WJOY, he made the following observations:

"I want to say some words on behalf of the beleaguered residents of Stowe. They feel sorely put upon by Mr. Ramsey, who wants to build a pig farm in that meadow.

"The people of Stowe are not really upset about the esthetics of a piggery. Nor are they really concerned about the negative economic impact such an enterprise would cause. Mr. Ramsey could sell his pigs to Harrington's for hams and help the local economy.

"No, I believe the good folks of Stowe are worried about something so ominous and evil that they dare not mention it—but I will.

"Remember, we are fast approaching the year 1984, and people are beginning to ask how far we have come along the trail toward George Orwell's dark vision.

"The good burghers of Stowe, however, have been reading another Orwell text, *Animal Farm*. And what happens in that tale of bloodshed, manure, and revolution? That's right. The animals take over—led by the *pigs*.

"What the people of Stowe fear, what sends them to bed quaking in their Nordica boots and silk long johns, is that the pigs will overturn Mr. Ramsey and establish a socialist or communist commonwealth right there in the Ski Capital of the East. That kind of thing could happen in the Peoples' Republic of Burlington, but not in Stowe!

"Well, I'm here to say to the folks of Stowe: Don't lock up your Mercedes or hide your Depression glass. If you are patient and let those porkers breathe deeply of that good gold-plated, bracing Stowe mountain air for a few weeks, then they will soon change into the humdingest, most genuine, four-star triple-A double-knit certified capitalist pigs you'd ever want on your slopes or at your cocktail party.

"And *no one* wants to change the Stowe town motto to: 'Two legs good; four legs better.'"

✓ A Vermonter in the U.N.

Believe it or not, the United States of America chose as its first ambassador to the United Nations a Yankee from Vermont, the only New England state without a coastline. When the former mayor of St. Albans, Warren Austin, stepped to the podium to deliver his nation's maiden address to an expectant planet, the crisis center of the world was then, as it is now, the Middle East. Austin approached the subject in true Vermont style—head on. He closed the subject with the ringing admonition: "It is time for the Arabs and the Jews to learn to cooperate in true Christian fashion."

CONCLUSION

VERN AND CHET WERE FEELING GREAT. The session was finally over—six weeks late. They had shared months of ideas and jokes, and Vern had made Chet a full partner in his story gathering. With two people on the prowl, they had quickly piled up the stories. Chet was outgoing, and he was not content just to listen. He had pumped legislators relentlessly to get more tales.

Chet had taken batch after batch of stories home and fixed them up. They had long stories and short stories—some of them were simple, some were complex. They were just about ready to let someone else look at them.

"When's the last time you primed the box?" asked Chet.

"About two weeks ago," said Vern. "There hasn't been much that was funny these last few weeks."

"Hey, don't be too down on the legislature, Vern. As Morris Udall said, democracy is like sex. When it's good, it's very, very good. When it's bad, it's still better than anything else."

"Well, I guess that's true," admitted Vern with a wry smile, "and I know I probably couldn't run things better than the folks around here do. That sure won't stop me from complaining, though!"

"I'm glad you stopped complaining long enough to collect the stories. You know, I think we've got enough to show to a publisher. Let's take a look at the stash."

Like gold miners sneaking back into a mine to see their lode, the pair headed down the gray stairs.

In the bathroom, everything sparkled. The tiles had been scrubbed, the mirrors had been cleaned, and the toilet bowls were blue with cleaner.

When they reached the cabinet, Vern was saying: "You know, I've got a few more stories stuck in my dresser at home that I ought to bring in. Did you hear the one about . . . What the hell!?"

Chet looked up. Vern had gone white.

"The stories . . . the box . . . it's gone!"

He looked at Chet. "You didn't pull one of your fast ones, did you?"

"Don't be ridiculous! You sure you didn't take them home?"

"No, I've never taken them home."

Chet stared down the row of stalls. "Damn," he said suddenly. "There's only two guys in the world who would do a thing like this . . . "